The Internet

For Beginners

By Web Wise Seniors, Inc.
The Computer Training Specialists

™

Web Wise Seniors, Inc.
305 Woodstock Rd.
Eastlake, Ohio 44095
www.WebWiseSeniors.com

Copyright

Trademarks

Windows and Internet Explorer are registered trademarks of Microsoft. All other brand names and product names used in this book are trademarks, registered trademarks, or trade names of their respective holders. Web Wise Seniors is not associated with Microsoft or any other product or vendor mentioned in this book.

Limits of Liability/Disclaimer or Warranty

Web Wise Seniors (WWS) has used its best efforts in preparing this book. WWS makes no representation or warranties with respect to the accuracy or completeness of the contents of this book, and specifically disclaims any implied warranties or merchantability or fitness for any particular purpose, and shall in no event be liable for any loss of profit or any other commercial damage, including but not limited to special, incidental, consequential, or other damages.

Sales Inquiries

For sales inquiries and special prices for bulk quantities, please call toll free 1 (866) 232-7032.

Introduction

"The best computer class I have ever taken!" and "I never knew that computers could be explained so well!" are comments heard frequently from Web Wise Seniors' students. Since 2000, Web Wise Seniors has successfully taught thousands of beginning computer users. Now, the same teaching methods successful in Web Wise Seniors' courses are found in this easy to understand book.

This book is not a reference for the Internet. It is a learning guide for people of any age who are unfamiliar with the Internet, but is especially designed for seniors who want to be skilled Internet users. It is like having a private instructor at your side as you walk through the basics of surfing the web. It is full of questions commonly asked by beginners in actual classes, followed by easily understandable answers which have already helped thousands.

You only get so far by reading explanations and definitions. You need to actually use the Internet to learn to use it well. This book will help you get started using the Internet by walking you through the basic skills Step by Step while answering your "whys" and "whats" along the way.

Web Wise Seniors teaches basic computer classes every day. WWS instructors have seen firsthand what works, what does not work, and what beginners want to know. We have drawn on our teachers' knowledge, skills and experiences to write this book.

About the Authors

Web Wise Seniors is a company dedicated to teaching basic computer skills to individuals over the age of 50. Since 2000, Web Wise Seniors has filled over 25,000 classroom seats throughout Ohio, and has quickly become a premier computer education company for mature adults in the Midwest.

Classes have been designed for seniors by seniors and are continually updated with the feedback of students. By becoming an interactive part of the senior community and working closely with senior organizations throughout the Midwest, Web Wise Seniors has been able to develop a unique teaching style and curriculum that have been overwhelmingly successful.

Since 2000, over 97% of Web Wise Seniors students have stated they would recommend the program to their friends and families. One hundred percent of affiliated teaching locations have been happy to work with the WWS program and, on a 4 point scale, WWS received an average 3.8 rating in student satisfaction.*

The same dedication and love of teaching that has made the WWS program so successful in the classroom is available for you in the pages of this book. Readers will find this book full of examples, illustrations and easy to follow directions. This is a teaching guide, not just a manual or reference book.

*Student satisfaction as collected through WWS classes and events (2000 – 2008).

About this Book

The Internet for Beginners is designed to be read in order. Readers should begin with page one and continue through the book as if they were actually taking a computer course. The sections all relate and build upon each other.

Readers should keep a computer close at hand while reading *The Internet for Beginners*. We recommend you read through an entire section and then go back and try the steps outlined in the section.

Keep a pen or pencil handy too. Take notes and highlight any sections that you feel are personally important. This is your computer book and the more personal references you make within its pages, the better this course will work for you.

Above all, please enjoy *The Internet for Beginners*. Read at your own pace and keep at it. You'll be an Internet wiz before you know it!

Meet Larry

Larry is the Web Wise Seniors mascot. You will find him throughout the pages of this book helping to "get the bugs out." Larry has been helping beginning computer users for more than five years now. He answers commonly asked questions sent to www.WebWiseSeniors.com, and often makes guest appearances in WWS publications.

In his spare time, Larry enjoys searching the Internet, e-mailing friends, and belly dancing.

Acknowledgements

We would like to thank the thousands of students that have challenged our computer instructors' minds in class. Your countless, and sometimes off-the-wall, questions and constructive feedback have made us better teachers. Without you, this book would not have been possible. Thank you!

We would also like to thank our family members for their insight, feedback, and support.

Credits

Authors
Michael Douglas
Stephen Pelton

Book Design and Production
Michael Douglas
Stephen Pelton

Proof Reading
Jean Pelton
Mary Pelton

Clip Art
Microsoft 2006 Clip Art Gallery

Screen Shots
Microsoft Vista
Microsoft Internet Explorer

Table of Contents

Table of Contents

Chapter 3: Internet Browsers!

Chapter 4: Searching the Internet!

Table of Contents

Chapter 5: Search Engines!

Table of Contents

Chapter 6: Favorites List!

Table of Contents

Chapter 7: History List!

Chapter 8: Changing the Home Page!

Chapter 9: Downloading & Installation!

Table of Contents

Chapter 10: Advertising on the Internet

Chapter 11: Viruses!

Chapter 12: Printing from the Internet!

Table of Contents

Chapter 13: Saving from the Internet!

Chapter 14: Privacy on the Internet!

Chapter 15: E-mail!

Chapter 16: Internet Yellow Pages

Chapter 1

Let's Get Started!

What You Will Learn in this Chapter:
✓ The Internet
✓ History of the Internet
✓ Information Available on the Internet

Chapter 1: Let's Get Started!

Section 1: What is the Internet All About?

What is the Internet?

The term Internet refers to a worldwide network that connects millions of computers and their users. Through the use of phone lines, cable, and satellites, over 100 countries and tens of millions of people have the ability to communicate and share information on a global scale. The Internet has been given many names to try to explain its vast reach. Some of the most common terms are The Web, The World Wide Web (WWW), Cyberspace, and Information Superhighway. Why was the Internet named the World Wide Web? Well, if you could view the Earth in its entirety, observing all the communication lines linking computers around the globe, the Earth would look like it was covered in a gigantic spider's web.

The Internet, or whatever term you feel comfortable using, is comprised of company, library, school, non-profit organization, and individual computers. Some computers are connected to the Internet for the purpose of sharing information and providing services, while others are connected to the Internet to search for information. Think of the Internet as a superhighway with roads connecting every destination in the World. Using your computer, you can connect to this superhighway and travel from destination to destination at almost instantaneous speed. In computer terms, these destinations are referred to as websites, and the superhighway is your Internet connection. These roads are filled with traffic consisting of people going different places. Some are performing research; some are shopping, some are communicating with friends, and others are doing everything else you can possibly imagine.

Every time you connect to the Internet, your computer is considered part of the Internet. Staying with our superhighway analogy, every computer that connects to the Internet adds to the traffic and increases the size of the Internet. When you disconnect your computer from the Internet, the size of the Internet shrinks and traffic lessens. People are constantly connecting and disconnecting to the Internet; therefore, the Internet's size is not fixed. The size of the Internet is always changing depending on the number of people who are using the Internet at any particular time.

You can travel as fast as the traffic allows on this superhighway. The time of day you connect will determine the speed at which you can travel from destination (website) to destination (website). Usually the Internet is slowest at the start of the work day, during lunch break, when the kids get out of school, just after dinner, and before bed time.

History of the Internet

The idea of linking distant locations with a network of communication lines has been around for more than a century. One of the first successful implementations of this concept was the telegraph, developed in the 1840s. The telegraph sent a signal of beeps over wires from one location to another. These signals were later standardized into Morse Code.

The Internet has come a long way since the telegraph. In 1957, the Soviet Union launched the Sputnik satellite and ignited a worldwide technological competition. In response, the US Department of Defense put together a team called the Advanced Research Projects Agency to figure out how to use its computers and technology more effectively. This group planned to link large universities, research centers, and government agencies together. They intended to create a network of computers which could be used to share information and also become a means of communicating from one geographic area to another.

The next step was to standardize the process of sending and receiving information. In the early 1980s, a set of rules called the TCP/IP network protocol was put in place to control how the information was sent. Also at this time, personal Desktop computer sales started to increase and the term "Internet" was coined by the Advanced Research Projects Agency.

In the early 1990s, a new standard for sending and receiving information was developed, called HTTP (Hypertext Markup Protocol). Even though the Internet was hard to use and contained mostly text information, the whole WWW system was finally made available to the public.

Chapter 1: Let's Get Started!

Marc Andreessen, a student at The University of Illinois, wanted to make the Internet easier to navigate. He created "Mosaic," a program called an Internet browser which made it easier to find information on the Internet. Mosaic also used more pictures and graphics which made it easier for the average computer user to use. Mosaic gained in popularity and Marc graduated, but since he had been a student during the program's development, the university retained the rights to Mosaic. After graduation, Andreessen started a company and, by the end of 1994, had created a new browser from scratch. He called it Netscape Navigator. By 1996, 75% of all Internet users ran Netscape Navigator on their computers.

With the success of Netscape Navigator, other companies, including Microsoft, began to realize the Internet's importance, power, and potential. Microsoft wanted to license Netscape Navigator to use with its Windows software, but Netscape refused. Microsoft responded by developing its own browser, called "Internet Explorer," which hit the market in 1995 as part of the Windows program package. The rest, as they say, is history. In 1999, AOL bought Netscape, but since AOL didn't use Netscape as the company's main browser, Internet Explorer became the most popular Internet browser.

What can you find on the Internet?

The Internet contains information on just about every topic imaginable. These topics include the weather, newspapers, stocks, driving directions, games, e-mail, recipes, jokes, health, nutrition, yellow pages, and much, much more. Every day the scope of the Internet continues to grow with new businesses and people offering more information, products, and services to the public.

Although people still use the Internet for research, it is no longer just a research tool. People use the Internet to buy and sell products and services, do research, find old friends and new romances, and as a means of communication. People from across the world are now linked together via the Internet.

It is important to realize that all the information on the Internet is *NOT* 100% accurate, true, or reliable. Everything on the Internet must be viewed with a careful eye, ensuring you are receiving quality information. Anyone who has the time, basic computer skills, and wants to put forth the effort, can place information on the Internet. Have fun exploring, but be mindful of what you find.

No one person, company, or government has control of the Internet. It is a public phenomenon which has no laws, rules, or governing body. It is owned by all people all over the world. Many governments have tried to police the Internet, but since every country lives by different sets of rules and belief systems, no one system has been mandated and the rules vary from one nation to another. It is important to realize that only YOU can control what you do or the way you use and act while using the Internet. We can only hope that if we act appropriately, it will rub off on others.

Chapter 1: Let's Get Started!

Chapter 2

Connecting to the Internet!

What You Will Learn in this Chapter:

✓ Connecting to the Internet
✓ Modems
✓ Choosing an Internet Service Provider
✓ Setting up Internet Service

Section 2: Connecting to the Internet

Connecting to the Internet

Now that you understand the basic structure of the Internet, you have a few choices about how to connect to it. If you do not have a computer, you can use a company, library, or school computer to gain access to the Internet. These locations will already have paid an Internet Service Provider to give their computers access to the Internet, so you can use their computers and get on the Internet for free. If you have your own computer, you can pay for the service yourself. This way you can use your own computer, at your leisure, to look around the Internet. The Internet setup process is commonly referred to as "getting connected" or "being Online."

In order to connect your computer to the Internet, you need a computer with a modem, a telephone line, and an Internet Service Provider. These items will be discussed briefly here and then additional information will be provided later in the chapter.

Most of today's computers come equipped with a piece of equipment known as a modem. The modem is a device, located inside the computer, which enables the computer to communicate with other computers. Specifically, when you connect to the Internet, the modem converts the information into a signal that can be sent across the telephone wire, like a phone call. The modem inside the receiving computer then converts the signal back into a form that the receiving computer can understand. Think of a modem as your computer's translator (English to French and then back to English) or in terms of computers (Digital to Analog and then back to Digital). Computers use a digital signal (series of 1s and 0s) whereas phone lines use an analog signal (sound wave).

Chapter 2: Connecting to the Internet!

You will also need to connect a phone line to your computer. Most people use the phone line already installed in their home, although some users have a second phone line installed just for the computer. Using a standard telephone line to connect to the Internet is called dial-up Internet service, which is currently the least expensive way to access the Internet. Other connection options, including Cable and DSL, will be discussed later in this chapter.

After purchasing a computer with a modem and hooking it up to a phone line, the last item you need to connect to the Internet is an Internet Service Provider, also known as an ISP. For a monthly fee, an Internet Service Provider will supply you with access to the Internet. Think of the ISP as the phone service for your computer. If you went to the store and bought a new phone, you would need AT&T, Sprint, MCI or some other telecommunications company to provide you with local and long distance telephone service. The same holds true for computers. You need an ISP such as AOL, MSN, PeoplePC, EarthLink, NetZero, etc. to connect you to the Internet. These companies provide you with Internet service for a fee. Basically, ISPs let the computer connect to their computer system which is, in turn, connected to the Internet 24 hours a day, seven days a week. ISPs are like the on-ramp to a freeway.

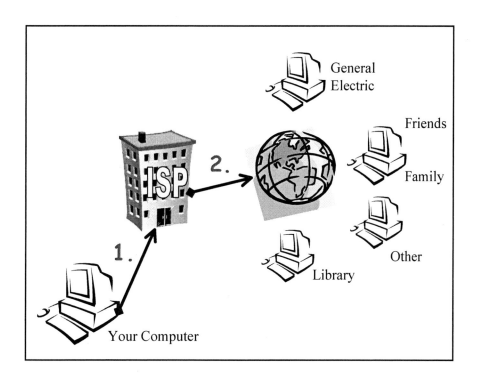

Chapter 2: Connecting to the Internet!

Once you have a computer with a modem, a phone line, and an Internet Service Provider, you can use your computer to call your Internet Service Provider to connect you to the Internet. So, put on your seatbelt, you are now ready to access to the Internet.

What is a Modem? *(A Semi-Technical Description)*

The word Modem is an abbreviation for Modulator-Demodulator. The purpose of a modem is to enable the computer to send information over a standard phone line. Phone lines are designed to use analog sound wave frequencies, like those created by a person talking. A computer uses a digital signal which is a series of beeps and pauses. To send the digital signal over the phone line, the modem turns these beeps into sound waves and then sends these waves across the phone line. The computer on the receiving end uses its modem to convert the analog waves back into a digital signal the computer can understand. In essence, it is the part of the computer that enables the computer to talk over the phone lines. If you do not have a modem, you cannot use the Internet.

The modem connection is typically located at the back of a desktop computer's tower (large rectangular box). On a laptop computer, the modem connection will be found on the side or the back. The modem connection looks like a phone jack. Desktop computers typically have modems with two phone jacks used to split the single wall jack between a telephone and the computer. You plug the telephone cord from the telephone into the jack with the picture of a telephone next to it. The cord from the wall jack is inserted into the opening with the picture of a phone jack next to it. As long as you are not on the Internet, you can use the telephone plugged into the computer to make or receive calls, even if the computer is turned off.

Section 3: Selecting an Internet Service Provider

Choosing an Internet Service Provider

There are a large number of Internet Service Providers (ISPs) and products. This section describes some of the options available to computer users. Remember, the ultimate goal of each service is to allow access the Internet and everything the Internet has to offer.

First, decide how you want to connect the computer to the Internet. There are three common ways to get connected: Dial-up, Cable, and DSL service.

Dial-up Internet Service

Currently, the most popular way to access the Internet is with a Dial-Up Internet service. This type of ISP uses a standard telephone line to connect the computer to the Internet. Dial-up is the easiest way to connect to the Internet because the computer is already setup to be connected in this fashion.

Dial-up utilizes the same principles used when making a telephone call to a friend. You pick up the phone, dial the number, and talk when the call is answered. The only difference in connecting to the Internet is that the computer is making the call and using tones instead of words to communicate. Because the computer is using your phone line, anyone calling you will receive a busy signal while you are connected to the Internet. As soon as you disconnect from the Internet, your phone will be available for regular use.

Chapter 2: Connecting to the Internet!

Companies that provide dial-up service include AOL (America Online), MSN (Microsoft Service Network), EarthLink, NetZero, and PeoplePC, just to name a few. You can find others by looking in the telephone book.

The cost associated with dial-up Internet access ranges from $9.95 to $23.95 per month, and is subject to change at any time.

You are probably asking yourself, "Why are there different prices for the same type of service?" Typically, different companies have different supplemental services supplied with their ISP connection. The more expensive ones may offer more services including name recognition, national access numbers, free 24/7 customer service and, hopefully, less advertising. Many companies are able to charge less if they do not have the extra costs associated with a free 24/7 customer support line.

To set up your dial-up Internet service, it is easiest to call your ISP and have the representative walk you through the setup process over the phone. Before you contact the ISP, connect your computer using a phone cord to the wall phone jack. During setup, you will be typing instructions into the computer so it can contact the ISP's computer system. Once setup is complete, you do not have to repeat the process. Just open the "Internet Browser" program and the computer will automatically call to get connected to the Internet.

Cable Internet Service

In addition to offering HBO and Showtime, many local cable companies now offer Internet Service. If you are interested in getting this type of service, call your local cable company to see if it is available in your area. How does Cable Internet Service differ from dial-up service? Well, instead of using the phone line to connect to the Internet, the computer uses your cable line. Sharing the same line will not affect your TV reception.

There are two advantages to Cable Internet Service. First, the cable line is able to transfer information faster than the typical phone line. Faster transfer time means that each page you look at on the Internet will load faster on your computer. Second, your phone line remains available. People will still be able to call you on the phone while you are using Cable Internet Service.

Chapter 2: Connecting to the Internet!

To use Cable Internet Access, the computer needs a special cable modem that you can purchase at your local electronics store. A cable modem generally runs approximately $100. Some cable companies lease modems to their customers. The cable modem usually plugs directly into the back of the computer's tower. The new modem will allow your computer to use the cable line. Before you buy a modem, call your cable provider to determine which modem you need. After the modem is connected, call your cable company and they will walk you through the remaining steps in the setup process. Because of the increased speed and convenience of cable Internet access, the monthly charge is typically around $40.

DSL: Digital Subscriber Line

In response to the high speed access being offered by the cable companies, the phone companies developed DSL Internet service. Digital Subscriber Line (DSL) Internet service uses a telephone line specifically designed for computers. Without the burden of phone traffic, computers can transfer files and information at a faster rate. Using DSL Internet Service also leaves your phone line open for regular phone calls.

To use DSL Internet service, the computer needs a special DSL modem provided by the phone company. The DSL modem typically costs approximately $100, but many phone companies offer rebates to cover part of the cost. When you purchase this new modem, it will come with instructions indicating how to connect your computer to the DSL service. Again because of the speed and convenience, the service typically runs approximately $40 per month, and is charged directly to your phone bill. Many phone companies offer discounts on DSL service if you sign up with a year-long contract.

QUESTION: What is Broadband?

ANSWER: Broadband is a term used to identify high speed Internet Access. Broadband enables a computer to transmit more data at a faster rate of speed. Broadband provides enough space (bandwidth) to sufficiently carry multiple voice, video, or data channels simultaneously.

Which Type of Internet Service Do You Need?

Generally, it is recommended that new Internet users start by using standard dial-up service. This way, while you are learning, you can save money and avoid the hassle of buying the new modem. If, as you become more experienced in using the Internet, you decide you use the Internet enough to warrant the extra cost for the faster service, you can switch to one of the other Internet services.

What to Look for in an Internet Service Provider

There are many different ways to locate an Internet Service Provider. If you prefer to use a local company, you can find a list in the standard Yellow Pages. Be sure to call a few of them to make certain you are getting a competitive price. You may also see many of the larger national services marketing their service via free CDs and computer rebates. One of the best ways to find an Internet Service Provider is to ask your friends. They will tell you if they like their service, what they pay, and whether they would use the service again.

Since you now know that many companies provide Internet Service, what should you look for in a provider?

1. Easy Setup
2. Local Access Number
3. Unlimited Usage
4. Convenient Customer Service

Section 4: Internet Service Setup

Easy Setup

One of the biggest frustrations of getting connected to the Internet is going through the setup process. The two most common ways to set up Internet service are via a CD or over the phone with a customer service representative. The CD or company representative will walk you through the steps instructing your computer on how to access the ISP's computers to provide Internet access. Calling the ISP customer service department is normally the easiest way to set up your Internet service. This way, you will be speaking with a person who can answer any questions you have during the setup process.

Typically, there are three steps required to set up the computer to access the Internet. First, choose a phone number (Local Access Number) from a list provided by the ISP. This number is used to contact and connect to the ISP's computers. Second, select a name and password to identify yourself to your Internet Service. Third, the ISP will require you to set up your payment method.

Once the setup is complete, you can get on the Internet. Each time you tell your computer to access the Internet, the computer will dial the phone number to contact the ISP's computers. Once the computers are talking to each other, the ISP's computer will ask your computer to verify who you are and your computer will verify your name and password. After your information is verified, you will be granted access to all the resources available on the Internet.

Local Access Number

The first and most important item to consider, when using a Dial-up Internet Service Provider, is the telephone number you will use to access the Internet. Your computer is going to make a phone call to contact the ISP's computers. If the number is not a local number, you will be charged long-distance fees during the time you are using the Internet. This can be extremely costly. If you call a local number, you will not be charged any additional fees other than your local rate.

During the setup process, the ISP will provide you with a list of phone numbers available for connecting to the Internet. It is your responsibility to review the list and choose a number that is "local" to your area. By selecting the number, you are accepting responsibility for your selection. This responsibility includes any related phone charges while connected to the Internet.

QUESTION: How can you make sure you are using a local number?

ANSWER: Once you have selected a number, the only definite way to determine if the number will be a local call from your home is to contact the telephone operator. The operator will ask for your home phone number and the selected ISP number. The operator can then tell you if it will be a local call. If the operator says the call will be long distance, contact your ISP to select a different connection number.

Customer Service

Customer Service is a critical issue when deciding on an Internet Service Provider. Look for an ISP which provides FREE 24/7 customer service. This will allow you to get help any time you are trying to use the Internet. Be aware that some companies do not provide 24 hour service, others charge by the minute for their customer support. The charges can go as high as $2.95 per minute for help. Limiting the amount of available customer support enables companies to charge less for the Internet service, but it can cost you a great deal of time and money when you do need help.

Choosing a Name and Password for the Internet

The Internet Service Provider will require you to select a name and password during the setup process. The name and password will be used to verify who you are. This protects you from others (e.g. children) using the computer to access the Internet without your permission.

The name you are asked to select is referred to as a Username, Sign-in Name, Login Name, or Screen Name. The name can be any combination of letters and numbers, but must be unique. If you select a name that is already being used by another client of the ISP, you will be asked to choose another name.

Often people will use some combination of their first and last name when creating a username. Keep the name you choose simple because you will have to remember it to get access to the Internet. If a combination of your first and last name is not available, try using a nickname or including some numbers.

Chapter 2: Connecting to the Internet!

For example, someone named John Frank Doe, who was born on 12/29/1921, might choose one of the following ISP Names: DoeJ, JohnDoe, or JDoe. If those names are not available, he might try: JFDoe, DoeJF, JDoe1229, Doe1921, etc. When you are selecting your user name, continue trying until you find one that is unique and easy for you to remember.

After selecting a username, you will be asked to choose a password. The password typically requires a minimum of 6-8 characters including both letters and numbers. Passwords are case sensitive. You will need to remember how you input the password, both capital and lower case letters, and enter it in the exact same manner every time. Choose a password you can remember, but which will be hard for others to figure out.

When you type in your password, do not be surprised when you see little asterisks appear instead of the actual letters or numbers. The asterisks prevent anyone around you from seeing your password as you enter it into the computer. If you think you have made a mistake while typing, erase the entire password and retype it from scratch. When setting up your password, the computer will require you to re-enter the password a second time to prevent typing mistakes. If you forget your password, you must contact your ISP to set up a new password.

QUESTION: Why must the username be unique?

ANSWER: The username must be unique because during the Internet setup process the ISP will create an electronic mailbox for you. This mailbox will allow you to send and receive messages through the computer. Your username will be the first part of your mailbox address. If two people had the same name, the mail could not be placed in the correct mailbox. Sending and receiving messages through the computer is called E-mail.

QUESTION: How is Internet service billed?

ANSWER: Internet service is typically billed to a credit card. During setup, you will be asked to provide a credit card number or your checking account information. Each month, you will automatically get charged for the service.

If you want to cancel your service, you need to call the ISP and cancel before the end of the billing period. ISPs assume you are happy with their service unless you contact them.

QUESTION: Does the Internet Service Provider you choose restrict your access to the Internet?

ANSWER: Once you are connected to the Internet, you are not limited in the information you can see or use. There are specific sites that require a fee to use their resources, but this has nothing to do with your ISP. Therefore, it does not matter which company you choose as an Internet Service provider; each one acts as a doorway to the same place. Once you are inside, you have access to all the same things available to others using a different Internet Service Provider.

Take a moment to think of the Internet as a local shopping mall. When you drive into the parking lot, you have many doors to choose from to gain access to the inside of the mall. The doors are the ISP and the Internet is the mall. It does not matter which door you use, because once you are inside you will be able to enter all of the available stores. The same is true for the Internet.

QUESTION: If you are on the Internet, anyone who calls will get a busy signal. Is there any way to get around this?

ANSWER: If you are connected to the Internet using a dialup Internet service, anyone trying to call you will get a busy signal because your computer is using the phone line to send and receive information. To fix this problem, consider one the following solutions.

First, you could get a second phone line installed in your home -- one for the computer and the other for regular phone calls. Second, you could set up a voice mail account with your phone company. This way, a person can leave a message which you can access when you are finished using the computer. Third, you could use a different type of Internet service like DSL or cable. These services do not tie up your phone line. Fourth, there are programs which will alert you if you are receiving an incoming call. These programs normally display the name and number of the caller and give you the option to take the call. These programs vary in price and can be found on the Internet (e.g. Callwave.com and buzzme.com).

Chapter 2: Connecting to the Internet!

Chapter 3

Internet Browsers!

What You Will Learn in this Chapter:
- ✓ Internet Browsers
- ✓ Opening an Internet Connection
- ✓ Window and Browser Layouts
- ✓ Browser Menu Options
- ✓ Toolbar Functions

Section 5: Opening the Internet Connection

What is an Internet Browser?

A browser is a program that enables the computer to display the text and graphics located on the Internet. The Internet consists of billions of pages of information, pictures, text, animations, etc. A page on the Internet is called a web page. A group of web pages provide by one company is called a website.

All of these web pages are built using computer code which tells the computer how to display the text and graphics. The computer code is called HTML (Hypertext Markup Language). The browser translates the computer code and converts the code into graphical pages. A browser is nothing more than a program used to display websites and help you navigate around the Internet. It translates each web page from computer language into something people can understand. Internet Explorer and Mozilla are two examples of browsers.

Opening the Internet Connection

When an Internet browser is opened, the computer will automatically attempt to connect to the Internet. The browser will instruct the computer to use the Internet connection which was set up with your ISP. Assuming you are using a Dial-up Internet service, the computer will open a window which can be used to start the connection. When you press the "Connect" button, the computer will dial the phone number to connect you to the ISP's computers. When a successful connection is established, the connection window will disappear and the browser will display your first Internet page. Getting connected to an ISP's computers is called "signing on" or "logging on."

Opening an Internet Connection: Step by Step Instructions

1. **Click the START button.**
2. **Choose your browser from the list (Ex. INTERNET EXPLORER).**
3. **Click the left mouse button.**
4. **Click the CONNECT button located on the Connection Window.**

Opening an Internet Connection: Visual Guide

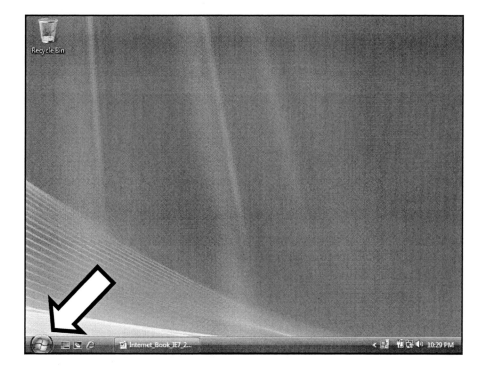

Step 1:
Click the
START
button.

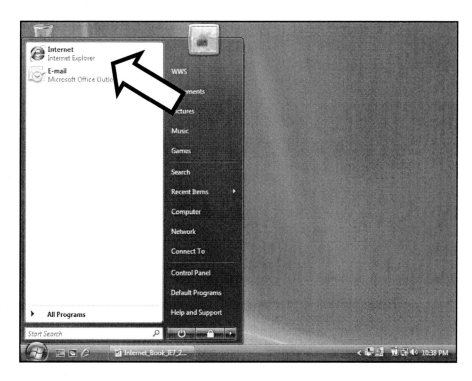

Step 2:
Choose a
browser.
(Ex.
INTERNET
EXPLORER)

Step 3:
Click the left
mouse button.

Step 4:
Click the
CONNECT
button located
on the Dial-up
Connection
Window.

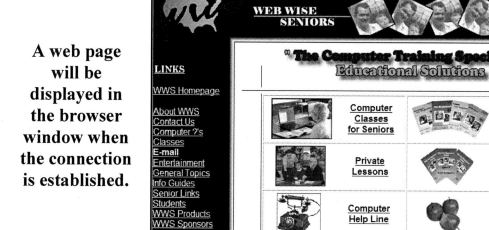

A web page
will be
displayed in
the browser
window when
the connection
is established.

How to Tell if You are Connected to the Internet

You can tell when a computer is connected to the Internet in two ways. If you look in the blue/gray taskbar in the bottom right corner of the screen, you will see the computer's clock. Once you are connected to the Internet, there will be a picture of two small computer monitors found next to the clock. When you disconnect from the Internet, the picture of two monitors will disappear or the picture will have a red X through it.

The second way to tell if you are connected to the Internet is to look at the browser. If you open the Tools option in Internet Explorer, there will be an option which says "Work Offline." If the computer is not connected to the Internet, there will be a checkmark next to the Work Offline option.

Section 6: Internet Browser Page Layout

Internet Browsers

All browsers perform the same basic function. They display web pages and provide tools to aid in the navigation of the Internet. When you become familiar with one browser, you should feel confident that you can use the other browsers. The screen layout, navigation buttons, and features are similar in each browser. Internet Explorer is currently the most popular Internet browser. It gained popularity because Internet Explorer comes standard on all computers running Windows. Other popular browsers are Netscape, Opera, and Mozilla. The example browser used throughout the remainder of the book is Internet Explorer, Version 7.

When you are looking around the Internet, you are "Browsing" or "Surfing." Located near the top of the browser window is the address bar, which allows you to choose where you would like to go while you are on the Internet. The address bar also contains the Back, Forward, Stop, and Refresh buttons to help you navigate around the Internet. Below the address bar is the command bar, which contains buttons that provide you options for the browser. The command bar buttons include Home, Feeds, Print, Page, and Tools. Each button plays an important role in making sure you get the most out of the Internet.

Other browser features include the Favorites List, History List, and the Instant Search Box. The Favorites list enables you to save website addresses. The History list keeps track of which websites you visit while you are using the Internet. The Instant Search Box line provides you with a location to search the Internet by topic. These items will be discussed in greater detail later in this chapter.

Remember, once Internet Explorer is opened and the Internet connection is established, the browser automatically displays a web page. This starting page is referred to as the Home Page. Typically, during setup, the computer's Home Page is set to your ISP's main web page. As you become comfortable using the Internet, you will be able to change your Home Page.

Chapter 3: Internet Browsers!

Typical Window Layout

Most programs, including Internet Explorer, open in a box called a "window." Every window has certain characteristics: the Title Bar, the Taskbar, Minimize button, Maximize button, and Close button.

The Title bar is located at the top of every window. The Title bar displays the name of the program opened in the window. The Taskbar located at the very bottom of the screen displays buttons corresponding to each open window. The Taskbar button will have the same name as the window's Title bar.

The Minimize, Maximize/Restore, and Close buttons are located on the right side of the Title bar. The Minimize button has a picture of a minus sign in it. Minimize removes the window from the screen, but does not close it. Your information is not lost, just hidden. When you minimize a window, the window is stored on your taskbar at the bottom of the screen. To retrieve your window, simply place your mouse arrow on the button that represents the minimized window and press the left mouse button once. The window will reappear on the computer screen.

The Maximize button is the middle button. This button has a picture of a big square on it. When you press the Maximize button, your window will stretch to cover the entire computer screen. After a window has been maximized, the large square box turns into two small squares. This change indicates that the window is at its maximum size. This button is now called the Restore button. If you click the Maximize button again, the window will restore itself to its original, smaller, size.

The Close button is located in the far right corner of each window. The Close button is typically red with a large white "X" on it. The Close button removes the window from the computer screen, removes the window's button from the taskbar, and turns off the program. Unsaved information will be lost.

The Address bar is located directly beneath the Title bar. Unlike past versions of Internet Explorer, in Internet Explorer 7, the menu bar was removed to streamline the browser. The Address bar contains two input boxes and the BACK, FORWARD, REFRESH, and STOP Buttons. These tools assist in navigation around the Internet. The Command bar is located directly beneath the Address bar. The Command bar contains options that affect information displayed in the window. The Internet Explorer window has five options: HOME, FEEDS, PRINT, PAGE, and TOOLS.

Address Bar

The address bar contains Internet Explorer's primary navigation tools. The address bar provides two input areas: the address box and the search box. The address input box allows you to type in the specific address of a web page you desire to see. The Search input box allows you to type in a general topic of interest and conduct a search to find additional information on that topic. Each of these methods will be discussed in greater detail later in the book.

The Address bar also displays the main navigation buttons people use to explore the Internet. These buttons are described below. To perform the given task, click once on the appropriate button. Clicking twice instructs the computer to perform the task two times. If a button is light gray, the option is not available.

- **Back Button** – Takes you to the screen viewed immediately before the current one.

- **Forward Button** – Takes you to the screen you were viewing before you clicked the **Back** button.

- **Address Bar** – Contains the exact web address of the website currently being viewed. (For example: www.webwiseseniors.com)

- **Stop Button** – Temporarily stops the computer from transferring information from the Internet. Useful when errors are discovered or you have reached the wrong site.

- **Refresh Button** – Reloads the website currently being viewed.

- **Instant Search Box** – Allows you to quickly search the Internet by topic.

Chapter 3: Internet Browsers!

Command Bar

The Command bar buttons provide access to Internet Explorer's primary tools. These buttons are described below. To perform the given task, click once on the appropriate button. Clicking twice instructs the computer to perform the task two times. If a button is light gray, the option is not available.

- **Favorites Button –** Provides a list of websites that have been saved on the computer for future access.

- **Add Favorites Button –** Allows you to save a website address on your computer (in the favorites list) for future access.

- **Home Button –** Takes you to the computer's starting web page.

- **Feeds Button –** Displays a list of Feeds available on the currently displayed website. Feeds are displays of newly updated web contents. An example of a feed would be new News Headlines.

- **Print Button –** Prints the page currently being displayed on screen.

- **Page Button –** Opens a menu displaying a list of options allowing changes to the way the current web page is being displayed (e.g. increase text size). It also allows you to save the content of a web page.

- **Tools Button –** Opens a menu displaying a list of options allowing changes to your Internet browsing settings (e.g. home page or pop-up blockers).

Home Button Menu

If you click directly on the Home button picture, the browser will automatically display the home page (starting page). Directly to the right of the Home button is a small black arrow pointing down. Clicking on the arrow will open a menu providing options dealing with your home page. The home page menu options range from displaying the home page to changing the home page.

- **First Menu Option** – (The name of the current home page is displayed as the first option in the menu.) Clicking on this option will display that home page.

- **Add or Change Home Page** – Opens a new screen (message box) which allows you to set the currently displayed web page as your home page.

- **Remove** – Allows you to delete a home page from the browser's settings.

Feeds Button Menu

Some new websites, such as news stations, offer information which is updated frequently. This might include special offers, breaking news, sports scores, stock quotes, etc. If the Feeds button lights up, it means the website you are viewing offers a feed. Clicking on the Feeds button (📶) will display the available feed.

Clicking on the black arrow directly to the right of the Feeds button will open a list of available feeds from the website. Next, use your mouse to select the desired feed. If the Feeds button is light gray, there is no available feed from the website you are currently viewing.

Print Button Menu

If you click directly on the Print button picture, the browser will automatically print the entire web page currently being displayed. Directly to the right of the Print button, is a small black arrow pointing down. Clicking on the arrow will open a menu providing additional print options.

- **Print** – Opens the print dialog window allowing you to select the desired number of copies and print range.

- **Print Preview** – Displays the web page as it will look on paper.

- **Page Setup** – Allows users to change how web pages are displayed and printed. Allows you to choose how a picture should be printed on the paper: vertically (portrait) or horizontally (landscape). It also allows you to change page margins.

Page Button Menu

If you click the Page button, a menu will appear providing options allowing you to work with the content of the page currently being viewed on the Internet. The options range from saving the web page to the computer's main memory to viewing the computer code the browser used to display the web page correctly.

- **New Window** – Opens a new browser window separate from the one currently being used.

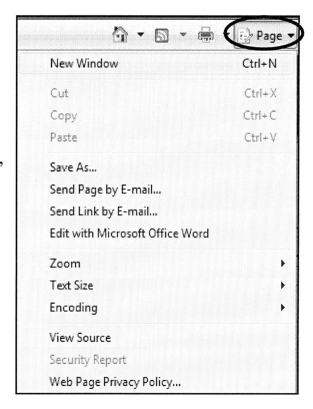

- **Cut** – Copies a highlighted section of a web page. (You cannot remove portions of most web pages. Only the person in charge of the web page, the webmaster, can edit it.

- **Copy** – Copies a highlighted section of a web page.

- **Paste** – Pastes text which has been copied from a web page into a word processing program.

- **Save As** – Saves the current web page and its contents to the computer.

- **Send Page by E-mail** – Sends the current web page through e-mail. This feature requires the use of Microsoft Outlook or Outlook Express.

- **Send Link by E-mail** – Sends a link of the current web page through e-mail.

- **Edit with Microsoft Office Word** – Allows you to view and potentially edit the content of a web page with Microsoft Word. If the web page has security restricting editing, this menu option will not be available.

- **Zoom** – Increases or decreases the apparent size of the entire web page including pictures and text.

- **Text Size** – Increases or decreases apparent size of the website text.

- **Encoding** – Tells the browser what language to use when decoding the web page.

- **View Source** – Displays the HTML code used to create the web page.

- **Security Report** – Displays any security certificates contained by the site. The Security Report button will not be available until you access a secure website, like an online store.

- **Web Page Privacy Policy** – Lists any restrictions placed on the current web page by Internet Explorer's privacy settings.

Tools Button Menu

If you click the Page button picture, a menu will appear providing options to work with the content of the page you are currently viewing in the browser. The options range from saving the web page to your computer's main memory to viewing the computer code which is used behind the scenes to display the web page correctly in the browser.

- **Delete Browsing History** – Opens new window that allows you to delete your Temporary Internet Files, cookies, browsing history, form data, and saved passwords.

- **Diagnose Connection Problem** – Helps you determine why your Internet connection might not be working properly.

- **Pop-up Blocker** – Blocks unwanted content and advertisements from automatically opening when you view a web page.

- **Phishing Filter** - Phishing is an illegal activity which attempts to trick a person into providing personal/sensitive information. Typically this is done by creating websites which look very similar to real sites (e.g. online bank) to acquire your personal data. The phishing filter checks websites for validity each time you go to a new web page.

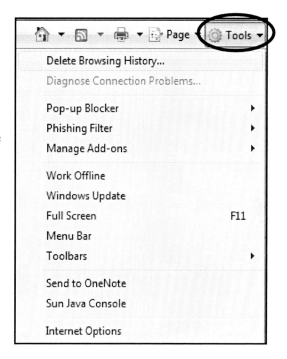

- **Manage Add-ons** – Multiple tools have been created to help personalize and enhance the Internet Explorer browser. This option allows you to find new tools, called add-ons, and enable or disable those you have previously obtained.

- **Work Offline** – Allows you to use the browser when the computer is not connected to the Internet. A check mark is displayed next to this option if you are viewing a website, but are not connected to the Internet.

- **Windows Update** – Tells the computer to check for manufacturer provided updates to Internet Explorer.

- **Full Screen** – Displays a web page using the entire computer screen. This option limits menu options and navigation tools.

- **Menu Bar** – An on/off switch for the gray menu bar located at the top of the browser window. The menu bar contains all the available features offered by the browser. Most of these options are also available by using the command bar buttons.

- **Toolbars** – Provides a list of alternative buttons which can be displayed on the toolbar.

- **Send OneNote** – If you have Microsoft OneNote on your computer, you can use this option to copy part or all the contents of the web page into the OneNote program.

- **Sun Java Console** – Enables Internet Explorer to use Java (a type of computer programming code) in the HTML web page code.

- **Internet Options** – Opens a list of options affecting how the browser displays web pages. These options include privacy policies, connection setting, and the Home Page settings.

Tabs

One of Internet Explorer 7's new features is tabbed browsing. In past versions of Internet Explorer, if you wanted to view two or more web pages at the same time, you would have to open multiple instances of the browser. Tabbed browsing lets you see multiple web pages on the Internet in just one window. The tabbed browsing concept will be discussed in greater detail later in this book, but for now, take a moment to notice the tabs between the Command Bar buttons.

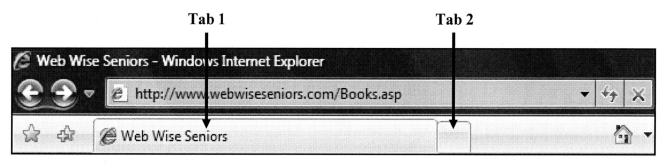

Disconnect from the Internet

When you are finished using the Internet, close the browser window. The computer should automatically ask if you would like to disconnect from the Internet. Select the **DISCONNECT** option. The computer will stop transferring data. Stopping the Internet connection is referred to as Logging Off or Signing Off.

QUESTION: What if the computer does not automatically display the disconnect message window?

ANSWER: If you are using a dial-up service, you can move your mouse down to the lower right corner of the screen and place it on the symbol of the two blinking monitors. Click the right mouse button. A list of options will appear. Place your mouse pointer over the **DISCONNECT** option and click the left mouse button. This will force the computer to stop communicating with your ISP's computers. If you are using a high-speed service, your computer is always connected to the Internet until you shut it off.

QUESTION: I do not want to use Internet Explorer. How do I find a different browser?

ANSWER: If your computer is running Windows, Internet Explorer is probably already loaded on the computer. If you decide you would like to use a different Internet browser, go to www.download.com. This website will have a number of different browsers available for downloading.

Chapter 3: Internet Browsers!

Chapter 4

Searching the Internet!

What You Will Learn in this Chapter
- ✓ Navigating Web Pages
- ✓ A Typical Website Address
- ✓ Website Addresses vs. E-mail Addresses
- ✓ Searching the Internet using a Website Address

Section 7: How to Navigate Web Pages

Websites and Web Pages

A website is similar to a "choose your own adventure" book. You begin reading from the first page, commonly referred to as the Home Page. The first page will have many choices (called hyperlinks or links) which will take you to subsequent website pages.

Hyperlinks (Links)

A hyperlink (commonly shortened to link) is often a picture, word, or a set of words which take you to a new web page. Links are usually blue underlined text, although they can be any color. Web pages typically have many links on each page. To use a link, position the mouse pointer over it and click the left mouse button. This will take you directly to the chosen page.

How do you know what is and what is not a link? When the mouse pointer is placed over a link, the mouse pointer will change from an arrow into a hand. The hand symbol indicates that clicking on the text or picture (the link) will take you to a new web page.

Chapter 4: Searching the Internet!

Links

Scroll Bars

Web pages are laid out in the same vertical fashion as ancient Egyptian scrolls. Therefore, there is often information located above and/or below your computer screen. To see all the available information on the page, use the vertical scroll bar located on the far right side of the window screen.

The scroll bar is made up of an arrow pointing up, an arrow pointing down, and a bluish-gray button in the middle. Clicking on the up and down arrows at the top and bottom of the scroll bar moves the information on your screen. Each click on the up arrow will move your viewing screen one line up your page. Each click on the down arrow will move your viewing screen one line down the page.

The button located within the scroll bar tells you where you are in relation to the total information available for viewing on the computer screen. If the button is at the top of the scroll bar, you are at the beginning of the document. If the button is at the bottom of the scroll bar, you are at the end of the document. Notice that when you press the up arrow, the button moves up the screen and, when you press the down arrow, the button moves down the screen. If you press either the up or down arrow and nothing happens, you may already be at the top or bottom of the document. To see if this is the case, check to where the button is located within the scroll bar.

HINT: Put your mouse arrow on either the up or down arrow. Press and hold the left mouse button down. As long as you hold the button down, you will continue scrolling up/down your document. This comes in handy when scrolling through a long document.

HINT: Another way to scroll is the "clicking and dragging" method. Place the mouse arrow on top of the bluish-gray button in the middle of the scroll bar. Press and hold down the left mouse button. While holding down the left mouse button, move the mouse arrow up and down the screen. This "click" "drags" the button through the scroll bar enabling you to scroll through your web page very quickly.

Practice using the scroll bar with the up and down arrows. Also practice clicking and dragging the bluish-gray button in the middle of the scroll bar.

Section 8: Website Addresses

Website Addresses

Every website on the Internet has a unique address telling the computer where that website is located. A website address is very similar to a house address. Each home address starts with a number followed by a street name. Each house address is different from the addresses of the other houses on the street.

Chapter 4: Searching the Internet!

This makes it possible for people to locate the house and for the postal worker to deliver the mail.

A website address typically has three parts. The first part indicates that the website is part of the World Wide Web. World Wide Web is abbreviated with three w's followed by a period (www.).

The second part of a website address is the name of the website. The name can be one word, a few letters or numbers, or a series of words grouped together. The only requirement for a website name is that it cannot contain any spaces.

The third and final part of an address is the "extension" at the end of the name. The most common ending is .com, but others include .edu, .gov, .net, .org, etc. The combination of the website name and the extension is unique. No other website on the Internet will have the same name and extension. If two websites had the same address, the computer would not where to retrieve the information.

As the Internet grows, companies have a harder time selecting unique website addresses. As a result, companies started registering used names with different extensions to make them unique. In the beginning, the extension used to indicate the type of website -- .com stood for commercial companies, .org for non-profit agencies, .edu for schools, and .gov for government sites. But, as time went on, companies and individuals began registering names and extensions, regardless of affiliation. All they cared about was that the address was not already taken. This has made the extension almost meaningless in signifying website types.

HINT: Website addresses may not contain any spaces. They are not case sensitive.

Chapter 4: Searching the Internet!

What Makes Up a Typical Website Address?

Examples: www.WebWiseSeniors.com, www.google.com, www.whitehouse.gov, www.yahoo.com

Part 1: www.
- o **www** stands for **W**orld **W**ide **W**eb

Part 2: Name
- o May **NOT** contain any spaces
- o Web Addresses are **NOT** case sensitive

Part 3: Extension
- o (.com , .gov, .net , .org , .edu, or .cc)

A website address is a direct link to a website. By typing the address into the Internet browser, you are telling the computer to go directly to the desired website. Website addresses can be obtained from television, radio, newspapers, and friends.

Internal Website Pages

A website is very similar to a book. They both have many pages that are divided into sections. In books, those sections are called chapters. In websites, those sections are called folders.

Just like you can tell a person to go to a specific page in a book (p. 243 of the Webster's Dictionary), you can also tell someone to go a specific web page. The specific address for an internal web page begins with the website address, followed by the folder name, followed by the page name. Each part is separated by a forward slash.

In the example **www.usatoday.com/travel/front.htm,** note that the first part of the address is the website's main address – www.usatoday.com. Typing the website address will open the website's Home Page. The "/travel/" indicates that the page is located in the travel folder (section) of the website. The third part, "front.htm" is the specific page's name. It is important to type in the exact address or the computer will not be able to find the page and will display a "page not found" error message.

Website Address vs. E-mail Address:

A website address is different from an e-mail address. E-mail addresses must include the @ ("At") symbol. E-mail addresses are used to send messages to, and receive messages from, individuals over the Internet.

    Example website address: www.webwiseseniors.com
    Example e-mail address: johndoe@webwiseseniors.com

Searching the Internet

There are two ways to search the Internet. The first way to search the Internet is to conduct a specific search. To perform a specific search, type the website address into the browser's address bar and hit the Enter key. This will take you directly to a specific web page. You can only perform a specific search if you know the exact website address of the site you are interested in viewing.

The second way to search through the Internet is to use a search engine. A search engine is the phone book of the Internet. When you type a topic into a search engine, it will generate a list of websites dealing with that topic.

Section 9: Searching the Internet Using Website Addresses

Specific Search

Located near the top of the Internet browser window is the address bar containing a white input box. The address bar generally displays the web address of the website currently in the browser window, but you can also use it to open a website by conducting a specific search. Make sure you know the exact address of a website or web page before attempting a specific search.

Chapter 4: Searching the Internet!

To perform a specific search, type the website address into a blank address bar. To type in the address bar, move the mouse pointer over any part of the white input box. Click the left mouse button one time. Everything in the input box should turn blue (it becomes highlighted). When something is highlighted, it indicates that the computer is focused on that item and is waiting for further instructions. Use the Backspace key or the Delete key on the keyboard to erase the highlighted text. Then type the new website address.

If you click the left mouse button in the address line and everything does not turn blue, you need to erase the text manually. A blinking line (cursor) should be located in the address bar. The cursor appears at the point you were at when you clicked the mouse. Use the Backspace key on the keyboard to erase to the left of the cursor. Use the Delete key to erase the text to the right of the cursor. After the text has been completely erased, type in the new website address.

Be careful to be exact when typing in the new website address. If any mistakes are made, the computer will not be able to find the correct page. When you finish typing the address, hit the Enter key on your keyboard.

Specific Search: Step by Step Instructions
1. **Obtain a website address from the TV, radio, newspaper, or friend.**
2. **Position the mouse pointer over the input box located in the address line.**
3. **Click the left mouse button one time.**
4. **Press the Backspace or Delete key on the keyboard to erase the highlighted text.**
5. **Type the new website address into the input box.**
   - **Remember a website address typically includes:**
     - www. followed by
     - The unique name, followed by
     - The extension (.com , .gov, .net , .org , .edu or .cc)
       - Example: www.WebWiseSeniors.com
       - Example: www.Google.com
6. **Press the Enter key on the keyboard to go to the website.**

Specific Search: Visual Guide

Step 1:
Obtain a website address from the TV, radio, newspaper, or friend.

Step 2:
Position the mouse pointer over the input box located in the address line.

Step 3:
Click the left mouse button one time.

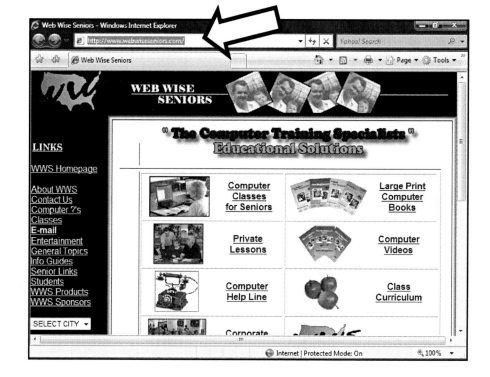

Step 4:
Press the
Backspace key
or the Delete
key on the
keyboard to
erase the
highlighted text.

Step 5:
Type the new
website address
into the input
box.

Step 6:
Press the Enter
key on the
keyboard to go
to the website.

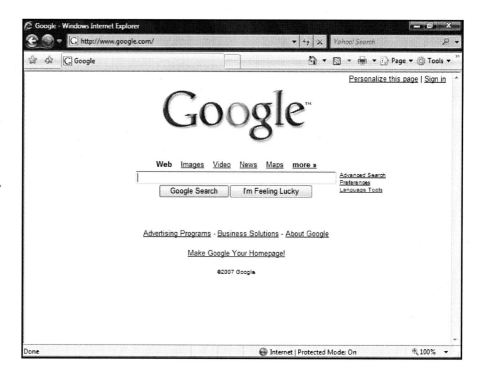

Result of the specific search.

For practice, repeat the Specific Search steps for a few of the website addresses located in the Internet Yellow Pages in Chapter 16.

QUESTION: What does the HTTP:// represent?

ANSWER: Take a moment to examine the address line. The computer automatically adds "http://" before the website address. Technically these letters stand for Hypertext Transfer Protocol. Basically, it enables the computer to transfer hypertext files (files containing links) across the Internet. There are other protocols, but HTTP is the most commonly used protocol on the World Wide Web. You do not need to type these letters. Your Internet browser knows they are supposed to be there and will put them in for you.

Section 10: Tabbed Browsing

Using the Tabs

One of the new features of Internet Explorer 7 is tabbed browsing. The tabs are located in the middle of the command bar and give you the ability to open multiple web pages in one browser window. Older versions of the Internet Explorer browser could only display one website at a time. If you wanted to open multiple web pages, you had to open multiple instances of the browser program (multiple windows) each of which could show one page. The Tabs feature was designed to make the process of browsing the Internet easier.

When you first opened Internet Explorer, the browser displayed the home page on the first tab. Take a moment to note that the name of the web page is displayed on the tab. Find the small rectangle located to the right of the first tab. This rectangle is the **New Tab Button** which allows you to open a new tab to display a new web page. If you position your mouse over the New Tab button, a small white piece of paper with an orange star burst will appear. This symbol indicates that clicking the left mouse button on the tab will open a new tab. Once the new tab is open, you can input any web address or view any website you can access.

As you open and use new tabs, notice that the first tab has not changed. To look at the information on the first tab, click your left mouse button on the desired tab. The selected tab will be brought to the front of your screen and the desired information will be displayed. If you want to have a third tab visible, position your mouse pointer over the New Tab button and click the left mouse button. A new tab will appear, ready for use.

Opening a New Tab: Step by Step Instructions

1. Click the NEW TAB button.
2. Position the mouse pointer over the input box located in the address line. Click the left mouse button one time.
3. Press the Backspace or Delete key on the keyboard to erase the highlighted text.
4. Type the new website address into the input box.
5. Press the Enter key on the keyboard to go to the website.

Opening a New Tab: Visual Guide

**Step 1:
Click your
mouse on the
New Tab
button.**

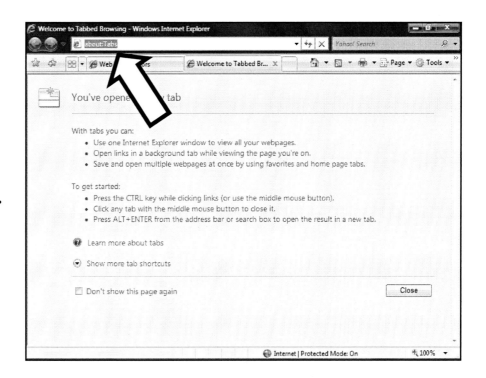

Step 2:
Position the
mouse pointer
over the input
box located in
the address line.

Click the left
mouse button
one time.

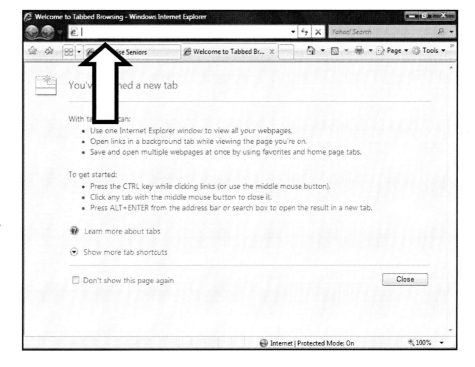

Step 3:
Press the
Backspace or
Delete key on
the keyboard to
erase the
highlighted text.

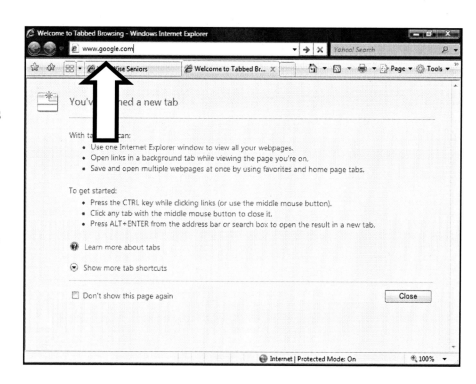

Step 4:
Type the new website address into the input box.

Step 5:
Press the Enter key on the keyboard to go to the website.

Result of the specific search.

Now practice flipping back and forth between the first tab and the new tab.

Chapter 4: Searching the Internet!

Click the tab containing the information you want to view.

Click the tab containing the information you want to view.

NOTE: If you want to close an individual tab, first make sure the tab is selected, and then click the small black X located on the right side of the tab. If you want to close all the tabs, click the red close X located in the upper right corner of the window.

Close a tab by clicking on the black X located to the far right of the tab.

Practice opening a total of four tabs and conducting specific searches for the following websites: www.webwiseseniors.com, www.google.com, www.yahoo.com, and www.msn.com .

Example of four tabs opened in one browser window.

Viewing Tabs

Once multiple tabs have been opened, the browser provides two tools designed to help select which tab is to be displayed in the browser's main work area. Directly to the left of the first tab is a black drop down arrow, called the TAB LIST button. The Tab List arrow opens a list displaying the names of the web pages currently open in each tab. To open the Tab List, position the mouse pointer over the black arrow and click the left mouse button one time. When the list opens, place the mouse pointer over the name of the tab you would like to view. The displayed tab name will be highlighted. Click the left mouse button on this option. The selected tab will be displayed in the browser's work area.

Click the TAB LIST button.

Click on the name of the tab you would like to view.

The second method for viewing a list of the available tabs is to use the QUICK TABS button. The Quick Tabs button is found on the command bar directly to the left of the Tab List button. The Quick Tab button has four squares displayed on the button. Clicking on the Quick Tabs button will cause the browser to show thumbnail (small) pictures of each tab's contents. To make a selection from the list, place the mouse pointer over the desired thumbnail and click the left mouse button. The selected tab will be displayed full size in the browser window.

Click the QUICK TAB button.

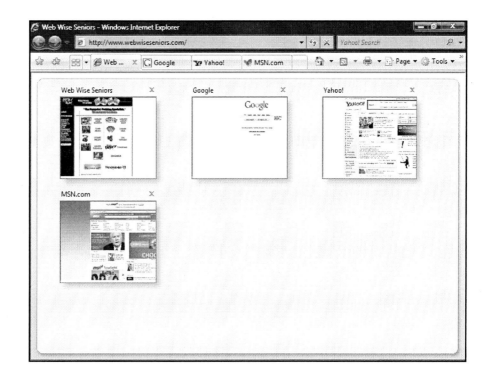

Click on the thumbnail of the tab you would like to view.

Chapter 4: Searching the Internet!

Chapter 5

Search Engines!

What You Will Learn in this Chapter

✓ Search engines
✓ Using a Search Engine
✓ Opening a Web Page in the Search Engine Results
✓ Filtering the Search Results
✓ Searching the Internet using an Exact Name or Phrase
✓ The Yahoo Search Engine
✓ The "Page Cannot Be Found" Error Message

Section 11: Using a Search Engine

A search engine is the second, and often the most productive, way to locate information on the Internet. A search engine is a website that acts like a card catalog (database) of the Internet. After you type a topic (word or group of words) into a search engine, it generates a list of websites pertaining to the topic. The list includes a brief description and a link to each of the websites.

There are many search engines available on the Internet. Currently, the most popular are Google and Yahoo. Search engines gain popularity for many reasons, including the number of cataloged websites, accuracy, speed of results, and ease of use.

Google has more than five billion web pages in its database and each is categorized by topic. Google produces a results list that matches your search terms or close variations of the words entered. Google then ranks each page using the number of external links pointing to the page from other websites and also by confirming the page relates to your search topic. Pages with the highest rank will be displayed first in the results list, and so on. When looking through the list, read the web page summaries taken directly from the text on the web page. This will save time and ensure that the page has the information you want.

Using a Search Engine: Google
The first step in using a search engine is to go to a search engine website. Open your Internet browser and type the website address into the address line. When you have finished typing, press the Enter button located on the keyboard. The search engine will be displayed in the browser window. In this example, you will be using Google's search engine. Google's website address is www.google.com.

The Google Search Engine Starting Page.

There will be a white input box on Google's starting page (Home Page). This input box, called the search bar, is used to enter the search term(s). Before you begin typing, the search bar must be activated. The activated bar will display a black blinking line (cursor) on the left-hand side. If the cursor (blinking line) is not present, position your mouse pointer over the white input box, and click the left mouse button. The cursor will appear in the input box. Using the keyboard, type in the subject on which you want information. In this example, type the word "nutrition." Once you have finished typing, either press the Enter key on the keyboard or click your left mouse button on the "Google Search" button located directly below the search input box. The search engine will generate a list of websites relating to nutrition.

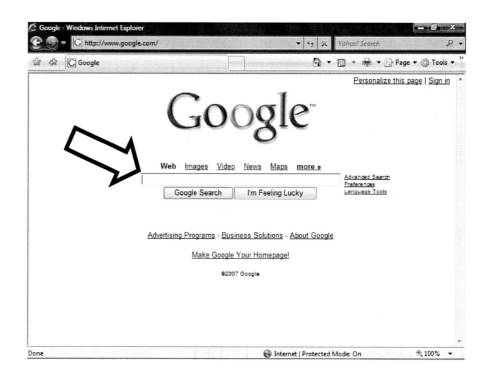

**Search Input
Box.**

Let's analyze the results page. Located at the top of the page, is a search box displaying the topic you entered. A second search box is located at the very bottom of the page, enabling you to enter additional terms or to begin a new search. Below the search box is a blue line displaying information on what Google's search accomplished. The left side of the line tells you Google searched the web for your subject. The right side displays the number of results found. Results one through ten are displayed on the current page, while the remainder (more than 20 million) will be listed on the following pages. If you cannot find a web page offering the desired information in the first few result pages, you need to focus (filter) the list. On the far right side of the blue bar, you will notice that Google takes a moment to brag about how quickly (less than one second!) it found the results of your search.

Chapter 5: Search Engines

Search Input Box.

Blue Results Line.

Web Page List.

Using a Search Engine: Step by Step Instructions

1. Open the search engine website (www.google.com).
2. Type the search term(s) into the input box provided.
3. Press the Enter key on the keyboard or click the Google Search button.
   - Other search engines call the Search button the Find, Fetch, or Go button.

Using a Search Engine: Visual Guide

Step 1:
Open the search engine website.

(www.google.com)

Step 2:
Type the search term(s) into the input box provided.

Step 3:
Press the Enter key on the keyboard or click the GOOGLE SEARCH button located on the screen.

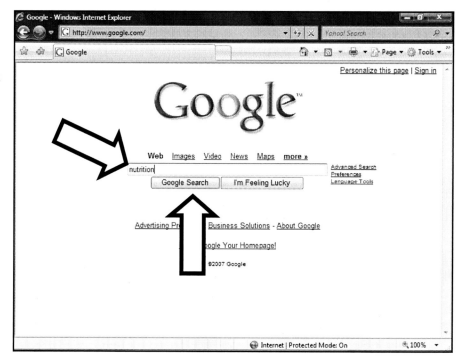

Chapter 5: Search Engines

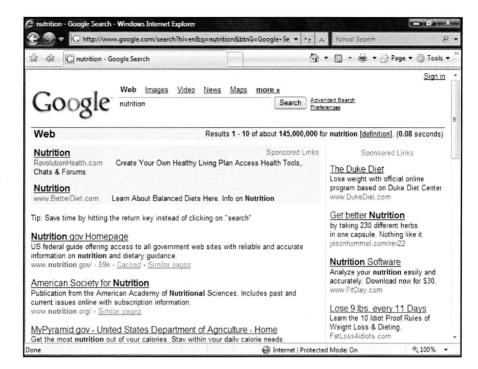

Search results page.

Below the blue line, the first ten websites will be listed. Each listing will include a description, the web page address, and a link to the page. The link is the top line of the listing (the blue underlined words). Move the mouse pointer over the link and the pointer will change from an arrow into a hand. Remember this is the browser's way of indicating a link. Click the link and the web page will be displayed in the browser window.

NOTE: The list displayed on the far right side of the screen is a list of advertisers. These companies enable the public to use the search engine for free.

Opening a Web page from the Search Results: Step by Step Instructions

1. Move the mouse pointer over the link (blue underlined words).
   - The pointer will change from an arrow into a hand.
2. Click on the link using the left mouse button.
   - The web page will be displayed in the browser window.

Opening a Web page from the Search Results: Visual Guide

Step 1:
Move the mouse pointer over the link.

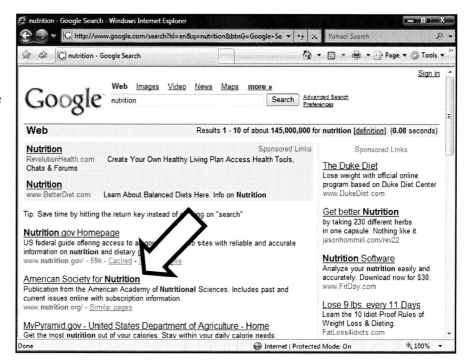

Step 2:
Click on the link using the left mouse button.

Open Web Page.

Once you have viewed a web page from the Google search list, you might want to go back to the results list and choose another website link. Use the Back button located on the browser toolbar to return to the page you came from. Each time the Back button is selected (clicked) using the mouse, the browser moves back one page. Depending on how deeply you have navigated into the website via the page links, you may need to click the Back button several times. Use the Back button to return to the Google search list. If you inadvertently go back too far, use the Forward button to move forward to the page you just returned from.

Using the scroll bar located on the right side of the browser window, scroll down the results page to view the other web pages in the list. Remember, to use the down scroll, position your mouse over the down arrow beneath the scroll bar and click the left mouse button. Each time you click, the browser will move down one line on the page. For practice, open another web page from the list, view the web page, and then use the Back button to return to the Google list. Scroll down the results page until you reach the bottom.

The first Google search results page displays the first ten web pages. To move to the next page of results, displaying results 11 through 20, use the "Next" link located to the right of the "Goooooogle" image. Notice the "Goooooogle" image has numbers located under the letters of the image. These numbers can be selected to move directly to the specific pages of results. Practice moving to the next few results pages. Try opening a few more result pages.

Moving to the Next Page of Search Results: Step by Step Instructions
1. **Scroll down to the bottom of the results page.**
2. **Click the Next link or click the page numbers located beneath the "Goooooogle" image.**

Moving to the Next Page of Search Results: Visual Guide

Step 1:
Scroll down to the bottom of the results page.

Continue scrolling down the results page until you reach the bottom.

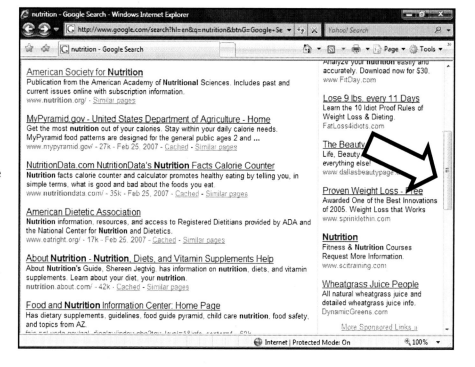

Chapter 5: Search Engines

**Step 2:
Click the NEXT
link.**

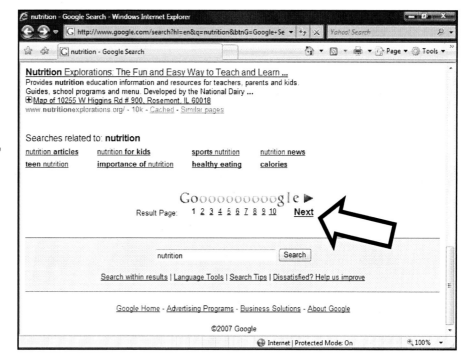

**Search page 2
displaying
results eleven
thru twenty.**

**For Practice:
Open another
web page using
the links
provided.**

**Use the BACK
button to return
to this results
page.**

Try a third time.

Scroll down to the bottom of the results page.

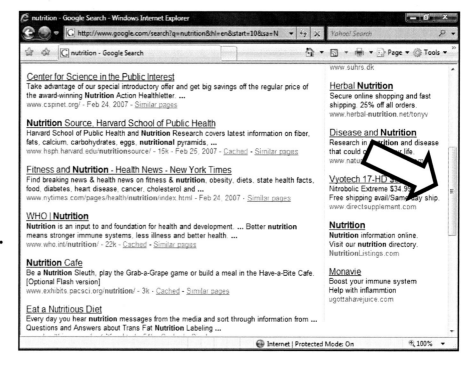

Click the NEXT link to move to the next page of search results.

Chapter 5: Search Engines

Filtering the Search Results

After looking through the first few pages of web page results, you might determine the topic you chose is too general/broad. The search engine allows you to add additional search terms (topics) to focus the search results. Adding search terms will shorten the results list and only display web pages which use all your terms.

To add other search terms, find the search input box located at the very top or bottom of the results pages. The input box (white box) will contain the original search topic (nutrition). Click the left mouse button to activate the input box for typing. The blinking line (cursor) will appear at the end of the original search term "nutrition." Leave a space and then type in the next search term. Be sure to leave a space between each search term. For this example add the word "diabetes." When finished typing, either hit the enter key on the keyboard or click your mouse on the SEARCH Button. The search engine will generate a new, more specific list of results using both the terms "nutrition" and "diabetes."

Filtering the Search Results: Step by Step Instructions

1. **Find the search input box located at the very top or bottom of the results page.**
2. **Position the mouse pointer at the end of the input box and click the left mouse button to activate the input box.**
3. **Add a space after the first search term and then type in the next search term.**
4. **When you are finished typing, either hit the Enter key on the keyboard or click your mouse on the SEARCH Button.**

Filtering the Search Results: Visual Guide

Step 1:
Locate the
search input
box located at
the very top or
bottom of the
results pages.

Step 2:
Position the
mouse pointer
at the end of the
input box and
click the left
mouse button.

Step 3:
Add a space
after the first
search term and
then type in the
next search
term.

2nd Search term:
"diabetes"

Step 4:
When you are finished typing, hit the Enter key on the keyboard or click your mouse on the SEARCH button.

You will get a new Results Page.

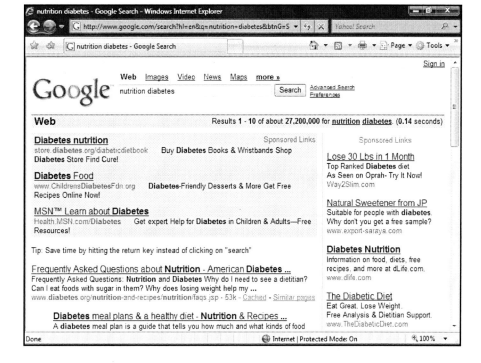

Look at the blue results line. Notice that when you added an additional search term, the results list decreased from approximately 145 million to just over 27

million web pages. After looking at a few more pages, add another search term and continue to refine the focus of the results list. For this example, add the term "recipes."

Step 1: Find the search input box located at very bottom of the results pages by scrolling down the page.

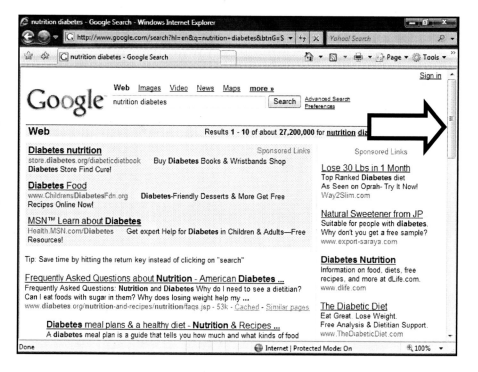

Continue scrolling down the page.

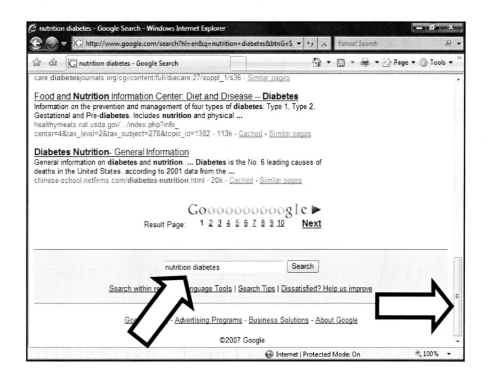

**Step 2:
Position the
mouse pointer
at the end of the
input box and
click the left
mouse button.**

Chapter 5: Search Engines

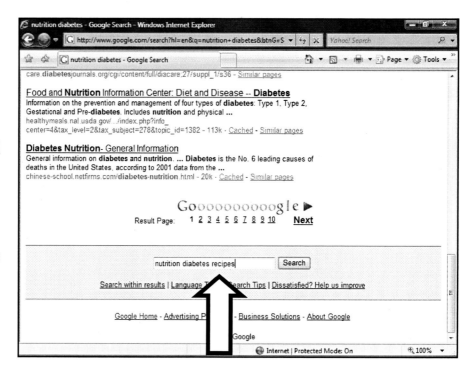

Step 3:
Add a space after the first search term and then type in the next search term.

3rd Search term: "recipes"

Step 4:
When finished typing, hit the Enter key on the keyboard or click your mouse on the SEARCH button.

You will get a new Results Page.

QUESTION: Can you start a search using multiple search terms?

ANSWER: Yes, multiple terms can be entered right from the start, but as a beginner it's best to start very generally. If the search is too focused, the information you are seeking might be filtered out. As you become more comfortable using the search engine, try searching using multiple terms.

Search for an Exact Name or Phrase
A Search Engine takes all the terms entered in the search input box and searches its database for each word individually. The search engine then compares the lists to locate web pages containing all of the search terms and displays the results.

A problem occurs when looking for a specific item using general search terms, e.g. John Smith. The search results may contain web pages with Louise Smith and John Jones, but not specifically "John Smith."   To ensure the search results provide the right information, place exact names and phrases in quotation marks. The search engine will then look for web pages with the exact phrase, "John Smith."

Section 12: Using the Yahoo Search Engine

Google is not the only search engine available. There are many others, but you will notice that many of the search engines have features very similar to Google. An example of another search engine is Yahoo. Repeat the nutrition search, but use Yahoo instead of Google. Observe the similarities and differences between the Google and Yahoo main pages, as well as their search result pages. To get to Yahoo, conduct a specific search by typing its web address into your browser's address line. Yahoo's website address is www.yahoo.com.

Specific Search: Step by Step Instructions
1. **Obtain a website address for a search engine (ex: www.yahoo.com)**
2. **Position the mouse pointer over the input box located in the address line.**
3. **Click the left mouse button one time.**
4. **Press the Backspace key or the Delete key on the keyboard to erase the highlighted text.**
5. **Type the new website address in the input box: www.yahoo.com**
6. **Press the Enter Key on the keyboard to go to the website.**

Specific Search: Visual Guide

Step 1:
Obtain a website address
(www.yahoo.com)

Step 2:
Position the mouse pointer over the input box located in the address line.

Step 3:
Click the left mouse button one time.

Step 4:
Press the Backspace key or the Delete key on the keyboard to erase the highlighted text.

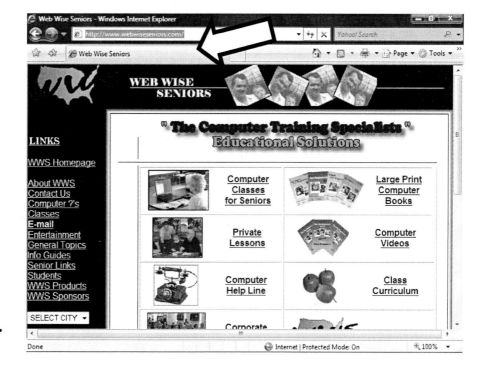

Chapter 5: Search Engines

Step 5:
Type the new website address in the input box.

Step 6:
Press the Enter Key on the keyboard to go to the website.

Result of the specific search.

Chapter 5: Search Engines

You have accomplished the first step in using a search engine. You opened the search engine website www.yahoo.com by completing a specific search using the website address and the browser address bar. The next objective is to use the search engine to search for information on the topic "nutrition."

Using a Search Engine: Step by Step Instructions

1. **Open the search engine website: www.yahoo.com**
2. **Type the search term(s) into the input box provided.**
3. **Press the Enter key on the keyboard or click the "WEB SEARCH" button located on the screen.**

Using a Search Engine: Visual Guide

Step 1:
Open the search engine website.

(www.yahoo.com)

Chapter 5: Search Engines

Step 2:
Type the search term(s) into the input box provided.

Step 3:
Press the Enter key on the keyboard or click the WEB SEARCH button located on the screen.

RESULTS PAGE:

Search Input Box.

Blue Results Line.

Web Page List.

Once the search results page opens, you will see a blue line telling you that these are the results from the search. Below the blue line, the first ten websites will be listed. Each list will include a description, the web page address, and a link to the web page. The links are the blue underlined words. Move the mouse pointer over a link and the pointer will change from an arrow into a hand. Remember, this is how the browser indicates a link. Click on the link. The web page will be displayed in the browser window. When you are done viewing the web page, click the Back button until you return to the search results page.

Scroll down the screen using the window scroll bar to see the remainder of the results. Near the bottom of the results page are numbers linking the first page, containing sites 1-10, to the second page containing sites 11-20, etc. Click the left mouse button on another number and the new page will be displayed. There is also a "Next" link which you can use to move to the next ten results.

Practice opening web pages from the provided results list. When you want to return to the search list, click the Back button located in the top corner of the browser window. This will return you to the previous page. Move to the next page of results and open a few more pages.

Open a Web Page from the Results List: Step by Step Instructions

1. Scroll down the results page. Find the desired link and place the mouse pointer on it.
   - The pointer will change from an arrow into a hand.
2. Click on the link using the left mouse button.
   - The web page will be displayed in the browser window.

Open a Web Page from the Results List: Visual Guide

**Step 1:
Scroll down the
results page.
Find the desired
link and place
the mouse
pointer on it.**

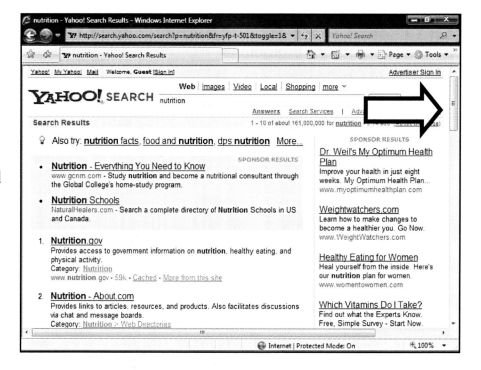

**Step 2:
Click on the
link using the
left mouse
button.**

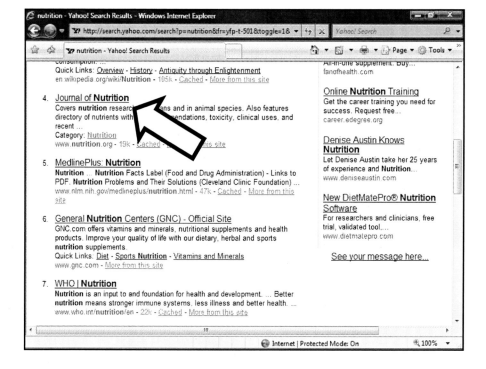

Step 3:
Click on an internal web page link using the left mouse button.

Step 4:
Return to the Yahoo Search Results List.

Click the BACK button.

Step 5:
Scroll down the
results page to
open the second
page of results.

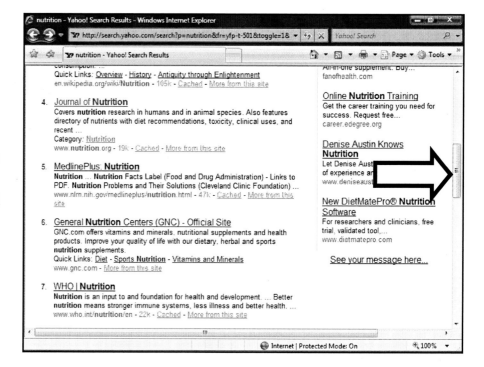

Step 6:
Click NEXT to
move to the next
page of search
results.

Search Results Page 2.

For practice, open a few additional web pages from the results list.

Section 13: "Page Cannot be Found" Error Message

"Page Cannot be Found Error"

If you are searching through the Internet and a "Page Cannot Be Found" screen pops up, do not worry. The "Page Cannot Be Found" screen appears under many circumstances. Some common reasons include: the web page was removed from the website, the address of the web page has changed, the website is temporarily not working, or the web address was typed incorrectly.

Chapter 5: Search Engines

As the Internet gets larger, it is harder for the browser to keep track of all of the pages and websites, resulting in more frequent "Page Cannot Be Found" errors.

If you experience a "Page Cannot Be Found" error screen, just click the Back button in the browser toolbar to return to the previous page. You may want to try to access the site later since the error may have been caused by a temporary Internet glitch. If the error occurred after you attempted a specific search, check the address in the address line. Make certain the address is typed and spelled correctly. Also, make sure there are no spaces within the address. If all else fails, try to locate another website which can provide you the information you are seeking.

Page cannot be found screen.

Chapter 6

Favorites List!

What You Will Learn in this Chapter:
- ✓ The Favorites List
- ✓ Adding a Website to the Favorites List
- ✓ Opening a Web Page from the Favorites list
- ✓ Organizing the Favorites List

Section 14: Using the Favorites List

Favorites/Bookmarks

Internet browsers have the capability to store and remember website addresses. Website addresses are saved in a list commonly referred to as the Favorites list or bookmark list. Saving a website address is called "adding a favorite" or "bookmarking" a page. This means that you do not have to remember a website's address to access it again; you can just save it to your Favorites list.

Add a Website to the Favorites List

To add a website to your Favorites list, first open the web page in your browser. For example, open the Web Wise Seniors website (www.webwiseseniors.com). Once the page is open, click the ADD TO FAVORITES button (star with a green plus sign) located on the browser command bar. A menu will appear providing the option Add to Favorites. A message box will appear in the middle of your screen. The title of the current web page will be displayed in the name input box. If you want to store the website address under its current name, click on the ADD button. To change the name, position the mouse pointer after the web page title in the white input box. Click the left mouse button. The blinking cursor will appear in the box. Erase everything in the input box by using the Backspace key. Type a new name into the box. Click the ADD button when finished. The new website will be added to your Favorites list.

When you are finished adding the new website, you might want to verify the website was added correctly. To view the Favorites list, click once on the Favorites Center button (yellow star) located on the browser command bar. The Favorites list will be displayed on the left side of the screen. To close the Favorites Center, click on the yellow star (Favorites Center button). The Favorites list will close. The Favorites Center button acts like an open/close switch and will open and close the Favorite list. Clicking on a website name in the Favorite list causes the web page to be displayed in the browser window.

Chapter 6: Favorites List!

Add a Website to the Favorites List: Step by Step Instructions

1. Open the web page you want to add to the Favorites list.
2. Click the ADD TO FAVORITES button located in the browser command bar.
3. Click the ADD TO FAVORITES option from the menu.
4. Check the Name Bar to make sure the website name is correct.
5. Click the ADD button.

Add a Website to the Favorites List: Visual Guide

Step 1:
Open the web page in the browser.

Step 2:
Click the ADD TO FAVORITES button located in the browser command bar.

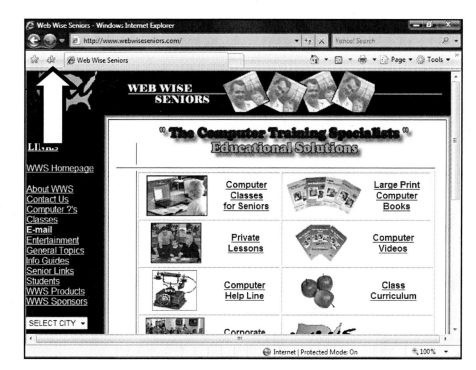

Step 3:
Click the ADD TO FAVORITES option from the menu.

Step 4:
Check the Name Box to make sure the website name is correct.

Step 5:
Click the ADD button.

Chapter 6: Favorites List!

The new item will be displayed in the Favorites list and the web page will be displayed in the window.

For practice add some additional websites to the Favorites list. Do a specific search for each of the following websites and add them to your Favorites list.

www.google.com   www.yahoo.com   www.mapquest.com
www.expedia.com   www.travelocity.com   www.aaa.com

Using the Favorites List

The Favorites list can be used to go directly to any website saved to the list. Open your Favorites list by clicking on the OPEN FAVORITES CENTER button (yellow star) located on the browser command bar. The Favorites list will be displayed on the left side of the browser. Place the mouse pointer on the name of the website you want to see and click on it. The browser will automatically open that web page. In this example, use your newly created Favorites and select the listing for MapQuest. Notice how the browser opens the page. Now, repeat the steps to select Web Wise Seniors.

Open a Favorite: Step by Step Instructions

1. **Click the OPEN FAVORITES CENTER button (Yellow Star) located in the browser command bar.**
2. **Once the list opens, click on your desired listing.**

Open a Favorite: Visual Guide

Step 1:
Click the OPEN FAVORITES CENTER button located in the browser toolbar.

Step 2:
Click on the desired listing.

Chapter 6: Favorites List!

The website is displayed in the browser window.

Section 15: Organizing the Favorites List

Organizing the Favorites

Over time, the Favorites list can become extensive and unorganized. Keep the Favorites list easy-to-use by organizing it. You can rename favorites, delete favorites, or create folders to group common listings.

The first step in the organization process is to open the Organize Favorites window list by clicking the ADD TO FAVORITES button (yellow star with the green plus sign) located on the browser command bar. A menu will appear. Using the mouse, click the ORGANIZE FAVORITES option located in the menu. The organize window will appear. The organize window allows you to rename, delete, move, and create folders. Creating folders enables you to organize the list by topic.

Chapter 6: Favorites List!

Earlier, you added multiple travel websites to your Favorites list. By creating a "Travel" folder, you can keep all of the travel themed Favorites together. Click the NEW FOLDER button located in the Organize Favorites window. A new folder will appear in the list with the name "New Folder" highlighted in blue. The computer is ready for you to rename the folder. Type the word "Travel." The words in blue (New Folder) will disappear and will be replaced by your typed term (Travel). When you are finished, press the Enter key on the keyboard to accept the name.

Now you need to place your travel websites into your new folder. To place a favorite inside the new folder, click the name of the desired favorite. The names of the websites are found in the box to at the top of the organize window. Click the MOVE button. A "Browse for Folder" window will appear. The "Browse for Folder" window provides a list of your Favorite folders. Click on the name of the folder into which you are moving your favorite. The folder name will turn blue. Click the OK button. The "Browse for Folder" window will close and the website name will be placed inside the selected folder. To move another favorite: first click the favorite, second click the MOVE button, third select the folder, and fourth click the OK button. When you are finished organizing the Favorites, click the CLOSE button in the bottom right corner of the "Organize Favorites" window.

Organize the Favorites List: Step by Step Instructions
1. **Click the ADD TO FAVORITES button located in the browser command bar.**
2. **Click the ORGANIZE FAVORITES option from the menu.**
3. **Click the NEW FOLDER button.**
4. **Type the name of the new folder.**
5. **Press the Enter key on the keyboard.**
   - **The new folder has been created and will be displayed in the Favorites list.**
6. **To move a favorite into a folder:**
   a. **Click once on the website name.**
   b. **Click the MOVE button.**
   c. **Click once on the folder's name from the list provided.**
   d. **Click the OK button.**
   e. **Repeat step 6 to move additional list items.**
7. **Click the CLOSE button.**

Organize the Favorites List: Visual Guide

Step 1:
Click the ADD TO FAVORITES button located on the browser command bar.

Step 2:
Click the ORGANIZE FAVORITES option from the menu.

Chapter 6: Favorites List!

Step 3:
Click the NEW
FOLDER
button.

Step 4:
Type the name
of the new
folder.

Step 5:
Press the Enter key on the keyboard.

Newly Created Folder.

Step 6:
To move a
favorite into a
folder:

6a:
Click once on
the website
name.

Step 6b:
Click the
MOVE button.

Step 6c:
Click once on
the folder's
name from the
list provided.

**Step 6d:
Click the OK
button.**

**Step 6e:
Repeat step 6 to
move additional
list items.**

Chapter 6: Favorites List!

Step 6e:
(continued)

Step 7:
Click the
CLOSE button.

The Newly Organized Favorites List.

Opening a Favorite Located in a Favorites List Folder

Selecting a favorite from a folder is very similar to opening a normal favorite. Once the Favorites list is visible, click on the folder containing the favorite. The browser will display the folder's Favorites below the folder's name. Click on the desired favorite. The browser will open the page. Practice opening the sites listed in the "Travel" folder.

Opening a Favorite Located in a Folder: Step by Step Instructions

1. **Click the FAVORITES CENTER button in the browser command bar.**
2. **Click once on the folder's name containing the desired website. The websites will be listed under the folder's name.**
3. **Click the desired favorite from the provided list.**

Opening a Favorite Located in a Folder: Visual Guide

Step 1:
Click the
FAVORITES
CENTER
button located
in the browser
command bar.

Step 2:
Click once on
the name of the
folder
containing the
desired website.

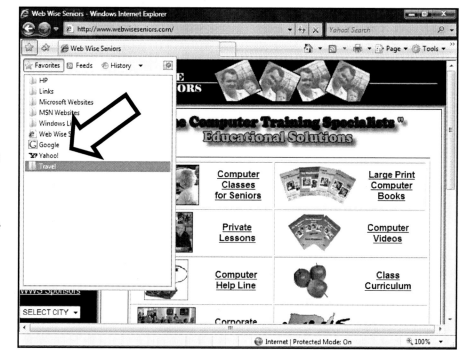

Chapter 6: Favorites List!

**Step 3:
Click the
desired favorite
from the
provided list.**

**The website will
be displayed in
the browser
window.**

Chapter 6: Favorites List!

For Practice:
Click another favorite from the list provided.

Locking the Favorite List

Many people prefer to lock or "pin" the Favorites list to the browser window so that the list is always displayed on the left side of the window. When the Favorites Center is pinned to the browser window, the window will automatically split into two sections. The left sections will display your Favorites Center/List, and the right section will display the current website. To make a selection from the list, click once on the name of the web page you desire to view. If you decide you would like to close the Favorites Center, click on the black X located near the upper right corner of the Favorite Center List.

Pin the Favorites Center: Step by Step Instructions

1. **Click the FAVORITES CENTER button in the browser command bar.**
2. **Click the PIN THE FAVORITES CENTER button (two rectangles with a green arrow) located in the upper right corner of the Favorite Center List.**
3. **To unpin or close the Favorites Center, click the black X located in the upper right corner of the Favorites Center section.**

Pin the Favorites Center: Visual Guide

**Step 1:
Click the
FAVORITES
CENTER
button in the
browser
command bar**

**Step 2:
Click the PIN
THE
FAVORITES
Center button.**

The browser window will split into two sections.

If the Favorite Center ____ much of the sc____ ____ze the section using the mou____ ____use arrow on t____ ____ight of the Favorites Center. Click and hold down the left mouse button when you see the mouse arrow turn into a double headed arrow. While holding down the left mouse button, move the mouse toward the left side of the screen. The Favorites Center section will to decrease in size with the movement of the mouse. When the section has reached the desired size, release the left mouse button.

Chapter 6: Favorites List!

Click and drag the right side border of the Favorite Center until the desired width is achieved.

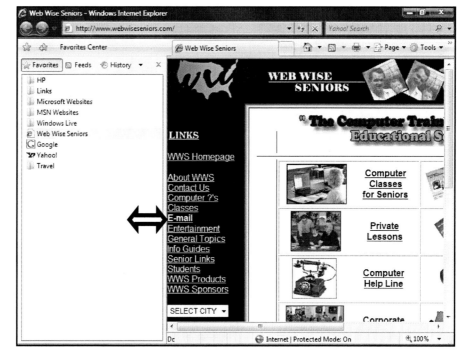

Release the left mouse button.

Step 3:
To close the Favorites Center, click the X in the upper right corner of the favorites section.

Full sized browser area.

Chapter 7

History List!

What You Will Learn in this Chapter:

✓ The History List
✓ Using the History List
✓ Erasing the History List

Section 16: Using the History List

Your browser is designed to keep track of the websites you visited while on the Internet. This is called the History. Why would a History be beneficial to a computer user? Well, the History list enables the computer to show you the links you have opened in the past and helps you easily return to websites you've viewed recently.

The History list displays the name of each website you have viewed. It keeps this list for approximately 20 days. The list is separated by days and weeks. So, if you were on the Internet on Monday, the computer will have a heading called Monday and will list of all the websites you visited on Monday. Not only does it display the website name (as a folder), but it also contains links to each page on that website you visited. To open the folder and view the page links, click the left mouse button on the website name. A list of web pages will appear indented below the folder name. To look at a desired web page, put the mouse pointer over the name of the web page (the pointer will turn into a hand), and click the left mouse button. The computer will go to that page. Remember, the browser is typically set to record your Internet travel for 20 days. After 20 days have passed, the oldest items will automatically be erased to make room for newly visited sites.

You may notice that sometimes links change color. Typically, unvisited links are blue while recently visited links are purple. This enables you to quickly identify websites you have already seen, saving you the time and effort of repeatedly opening the same websites.

You can also use the History list to see the websites your computer has been to when other people have used it. For example, you can use the History list to find out what websites your grandson went to while he was visiting or what your spouse is buying (on the Internet) for your birthday. We are not suggesting you spy on others, but the option is available if you need it. But, remember, if you can spy on someone in your household, someone in your household can spy on you.

Chapter 7: History List!

Opening the History List

The history list is part of the Favorites Center. Open the History list by first clicking on the FAVORITES CENTER button (yellow star) and then clicking your mouse on the HISTORY button located at the top of the Favorites Center list. The History button is also usually represented by an image of a clock or sundial. The Favorites Center will change to display the History list.

Using the History List: Step by Step Instructions

1. Click the FAVORITES CENTER button located in the command bar.
2. Click the HISTORY button located at the top of the Favorites Center section.
3. Click on the heading displaying the day or week you want to view.
4. Click the website name to display a detailed list of the web pages visited.
5. Click the web page name to open the page in the browser window.

Using the History List: Visual Guide

Step 1: Click the FAVORITES CENTER button located in the command bar.

Chapter 7: History List!

**Step 2:
Click the
HISTORY
button.**

**Step 3:
Click on the
heading
displaying the
day or week you
want to view.**

Step 4:
Click the website name to display a detailed list of the web pages visited.

Step 5:
Click the web page name to open the page in the browser window.

Chapter 7: History List!

The web page is now open in the window on the right side.

Practice

Step 1: Click the FAVORITES CENTER button.

Step 2: Click the HISTORY button.

Practice

Step 3:
Click the
website name to
display a
detailed list of
the web pages
visited.

Step 4:
Click the web
page name to
open the page in
the browser
window.

The web page is
now open in the
window on the
right side.

Section 17: Erasing the History List

Erasing the History List

There may be times you wish to erase the History list. Let's say you were buying a gift for someone over the Internet and you did not want to risk them finding out. Erasing the History list ensures someone cannot discover where you have gone on the Internet.

To erase the History list, first locate the TOOLS button on the command bar. Click once on the TOOLS button to open the menu. Move the mouse pointer down the menu list and position it over the DELETE BROWSING HISTORY option. It will turn blue. Clicking the left mouse button opens the Internet browsing history. A new window will appear providing six options including "Temporary Internet Files," "Cookies," "History," "Form Data," "Passwords," and the "DELETE ALL" button.

To delete a specific category of information, click the DELETE button directly to the right of the desired option. If you want to erase your entire browsing history, click the DELETE ALL button at the bottom of the window. A message box will appear to verify the delete. Click the YES button and the specified data will be erased. Once you have erased the desired data, click the CLOSE button to remove the Delete Browsing History window. To make sure the list was erased, open the Favorites Center to view the History list.

History List Delete Options

Temporary Internet Files: The browser automatically stores web pages you visit in a folder called the "Temporary Internet Files." Storing websites speeds up how quickly a page is displayed, for those sites you have visited in the past, because your computer pulls the information from your computer's memory instead of starting over on the Internet. The DELETE FILES button will delete all the files stored in the Temporary Internet Files Folder.

Chapter 7: History List!

Cookies: Cookies are small files websites put on a computer to store your personal preferences (e.g. zip code). The website then uses the cookie, the next time you return to the website, to quickly customize how the information is displayed. The DELETE COOKIES button will delete all the cookies stored on the computer.

History: History is a list of the websites you have visited on the Internet. The DELETE HISTORY button will delete the list of websites stored in the computer.

Forms Data: Forms are used on the Internet to provide websites your personal information (e.g. home address when purchasing an item from an online store). The form data is saved in your computer's memory so the next time you need to provide a company the same information, the computer will automatically fill in the data from its past memory. The DELETE FORMS button will delete all the form information stored in the computer.

Passwords: Many websites and other parts of the Internet require you to use a password to gain access to the desired information (e.g. e-mail, online banking). When you first type the password, the computer will ask you if you want to store the password for future use. If you say Yes, the password is then stored in the computer's memory until needed in the future. The DELETE PASSWORDS button will delete all the passwords stored in computer's memory.

DELETE ALL: Erases the computer's entire browsing history, but doesn't affect your Favorites. The DELETE FILES button will delete all the files stored in the Temporary Internet Files Folder.

Erasing the History List: Step by Step Instructions
1. **Click the TOOLS button.**
2. **Click the DELETE BROWSING HISTORY option.**
3. **Click either the DELETE button located next to the specific part of the browsing history you would like to delete or the DELETE ALL button.**
4. **Click the YES button on the message window.**
5. **Click the CLOSE button.**

Erasing the History List: Visual Guide

**Step 1:
Click the
TOOLS button.**

**Step 2:
Click the
DELETE
BROWSING
HISTORY
option.**

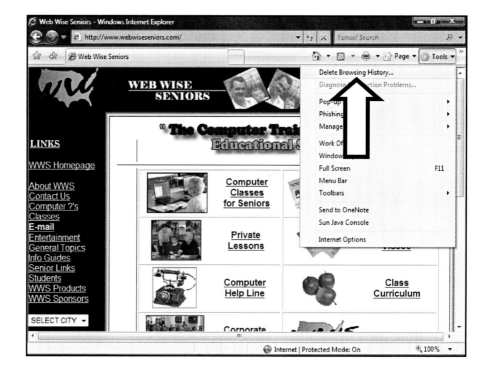

Step 3:
Click either the DELETE button located next to the specific part of the browsing history you would like to delete or the DELETE ALL button.

Step 4:
Click the YES button on the message window.

**Step 5:
Click the
CLOSE button.**

Now, verify that the history list was erased.

**Step 1:
Click the
FAVORITES
CENTER
button (the
yellow star).**

Chapter 7: History List!

The History list is empty.

Chapter 7: History List!

Chapter 8

Changing the Home Page!

What You Will Learn in this Chapter
- ✓ A Home Page
- ✓ Changing the Browser's Home Page

Section 18: Browser Home Page

Once you have connected to the Internet and have opened your browser, most browsers automatically display a web page. This first page is called the Home Page. During setup, Internet Service Providers typically set the computer to open to their main web page. If your friend has a different ISP, your starting page (Home Page) will be different from your friend's Home Page.

As you become familiar with different websites, you may decide to change your Home Page. You can set your Home Page to any site you like. You may want to set the Home Page to a site that provides one of the following services: news, weather, search engines, e-mail, or to a site providing useful resources.

To set the Home Page, find the TOOLS button located on the browser's command bar. Click once on the TOOLS button to open the menu. Move the mouse pointer down the menu list and position it over the last selection, INTERNET OPTIONS, which will turn blue. Click the left mouse button to open the Internet Options window. Located at the top of the window is the heading Home Page.

There are four ways to set your the Home Page. If you know the web address of the website you want as your Home Page, type the address in the input box provided. Another option is to open your browser to the web page you want as your Home Page, and click the USE CURRENT button. The web page being displayed in your browser window will be set as your Home Page. A third option is to click the USE DEFAULT button. The computer manufacturer's website will be set as the Home Page. Finally, if you do not like any of the above options, you can click the USE BLANK button. The browser will always begin with a blank Home Page. When you have changed your Home Page, click the OK button to close the Internet Options window.

Chapter 8: Changing the Home Page!

If you change the browser's Home Page, the HOME button located on the browser toolbar will also be affected. No matter where you are on the Internet, clicking the HOME button in the toolbar will take you directly to the website you selected as your browser's Home Page.

Changing the Home Page: Step by Step Instructions
1. **Click the TOOLS button.**
2. **Click INTERNET OPTIONS.**
3. **Type the new website address in the input box provided.**
4. **Click the OK button.**

Changing the Home Page: Visual Guide

**Step 1:
Click the
TOOLS button.**

Chapter 8: Changing the Home Page!

**Step 2:
Click
INTERNET
OPTIONS.**

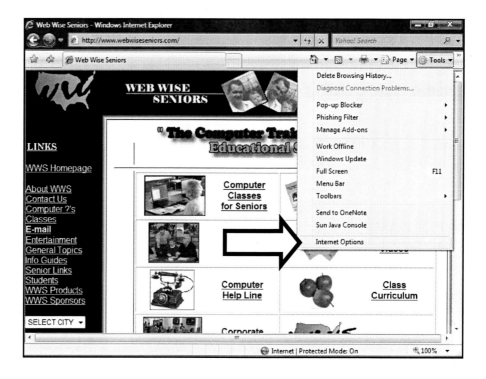

**Step 3:
Type the new
website address
in the input box
provided.**

Step 4:
Click the OK
button.

Chapter 8: Changing the Home Page!

Internet Explorer allows you to set multiple home pages. Each home page will open on a new tab. To add an additional home page, open the Internet Options window. Click at the end of the first Home Page address listing, press the Enter key on the keyboard, and then type the website address of the second desired home page under the first address. Once you are finished typing, click the OK button and the second home page will open on a new tab.

**Step 1:
Click the
TOOLS button.**

Step2:
Click at the end
of the first home
page listing.

Step 3:
Press the
ENTER key on
the keyboard.

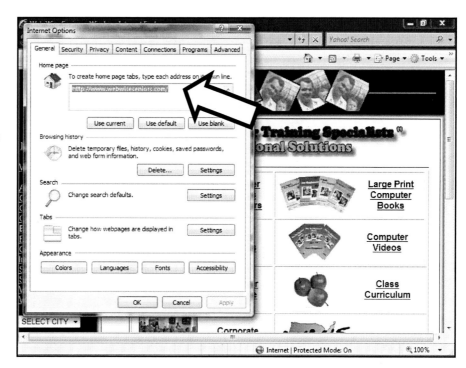

Step 4:
Type the
website address
in the input box
provided.

Step 5:
Click the OK
button.

Each home page
will be
displayed on its
own tab.

Click the tab
referencing the
home page you
would like to
see.

For Practice: Click the tab referencing the other home page.

Chapter 8: Changing the Home Page!

Chapter 9

Downloading & Installation!

What You Will Learn in this Chapter
- ✓ Downloading
- ✓ Downloading from the Internet
- ✓ Installation
- ✓ Installing a New Program
- ✓ Opening a Newly Installed Program
- ✓ Downloading and Installing Adobe® Reader and RealPlayer®

Section 19: Downloading from the Internet

While you are on the Internet, you may find a program, picture, song, etc. that you permanently want to have on your computer. Taking something from the Internet and placing in on your computer is called Downloading. Music, pictures, programs, and videos are just a few of the items people download. The download process is similar to going to a website and clicking on a link. Instead of the link taking you to another web page, it opens a window prompting you to run, open, or save the item (file) you want to download.

The first step in the downloading process is to find the item you wish to download. People often become aware of downloadable items via TV, magazines, radio, e-mail, or by word of mouth. In order to find a specific item, you may want to look at the website of the company which created the program/item. Once you have located the desired item, you will need to tell your computer that you would like to download it. Most websites which have downloads available will provide instructions for downloading. Most downloadable items will have links next to the item saying "Get It Now" or "Download Now". Click on this link to begin the process. After you have clicked the link to start the download, a window will appear prompting you to run, open, or save the file.

Large files, such as programs/software, typically utilize download management programs to guide the download process. The RUN option instructs the computer to launch a download management program to track the progress of the download. The OPEN option can be used to temporarily view a file from its original location. This option is used primary when downloading pictures or documents. The Save option allows you to permanently store an item on your computer. Select SAVE to download a copy of the item onto the computer. When downloading a program, use the RUN option. To download anything else, the SAVE option is normally the correct choice.

Chapter 9: Downloading & Installation!

Downloading a Computer Program

If you are going to download a program off the Internet, select the RUN option when prompted. When you choose RUN, the computer will automatically begin the download. The first item transferred to the computer is a small download management program which helps guide you through the process of transferring and loading the new program. The download management software keeps track of the entire download process and will update you on the progress. Depending on the size of the file, your Internet connection, and your computer capacity, the download time will vary.

Downloading a Computer File

If you are going to download pictures, documents, or other small files, choose the SAVE option when prompted. When you choose SAVE, the computer will open the Save window. From this point, the download process is identical to saving a document in a word processing program like Word. There are three steps in the process. First, tell the computer where you want to save the file. Second, give the file a name. Third, click the SAVE button.

The first step tells the computer where you want to save the file. At the top of the save screen, is a white box and a gray arrow pointing down. This gray arrow is called a drop down arrow. It tells the computer user that there are more options offered within the input box. When you click the gray arrow, a list will appear displaying the locations into which you can save your file. This box should say "Desktop." If it does not, click on the drop down arrow and, once you have opened the list, place your mouse pointer over the option DESKTOP. It will turn blue. To make the selection, click the left mouse button. The drop down list will close and "Desktop" will be displayed in the Save In: box.

The second step is to choose a name for the file. Located near the bottom of the save screen, you will see the heading "File Name:." To the right of the heading File Name: is a white input box containing the name of the file to be downloaded. The name in the input box is the website's suggested name. If the suggestion looks good, go on to the third and final step.

The final step in the save process is to click the SAVE button located on the bottom right side of the save screen. When you click the SAVE button, the computer will close the save screen. The file will begin transferring (downloading) and will be saved to the computer's main memory. A progress bar will appear on the screen showing the transfer. The window will tell you when the transfer is complete. After the file is completely downloaded, click the CLOSE button on the progress window.

The download process is complete. Now, you need to locate the file on the computer and open it. Since you saved the file to the Desktop, that is where the downloaded program will appear. Minimize your browser window and look at the desktop. You will see a new icon (picture) representing the file. Double click the icon to open the file. If the downloaded file is music or video, the computer will automatically play the item. If the downloaded file is a letter or document, the computer will open the item in your word processing program.

If the downloaded file is a program, double clicking on the icon automatically starts the installation process. The installation process instructs the computer how to set up and use the new program. An installation window will appear and walk you through the setup steps. We will discuss Installing later in the chapter. Once the downloaded file is installed, you can open the program using the Start menu.

Downloading is similar to ordering from a catalog. First, you find the desired item in the catalog and call the company to place the order. The company then ships the item to you. After the mail carrier delivers the package, you open it to view the item. Depending on what you order, the item might need to be assembled before use. Assembling an item can be compared to installing a downloaded program.

Adobe® Acrobat Reader

Download the program "Adobe Reader," also known as "Adobe Acrobat Reader," to experience the downloading process. Adobe Reader is a free program available to anyone on the Internet. Basically, Adobe Reader is a program which allows people to read and print complicated documents (called .pdf files). You will often see applications and tax forms in this format. To open the website, do a specific search using the website address www.adobe.com.

Chapter 9: Downloading & Installation!

Downloading a Program from the Internet: Step by Step Instructions

1. Find the program on the Internet you would like to add to the computer.
2. Click the link for downloading the object. It should say something similar to DOWNLOAD or GET IT NOW.
3. The information bar and a warning message will appear to inform you a program is accessing your computer.
   - Click the CLOSE button.
   - Click on the Information Bar. A submenu will open.
   - Click the option DOWNLOAD FILE.
4. Choose the option RUN.
   - The information bar and message box will appear to inform you a program is trying to access your computer.
   - Close the message box and click on the Information Bar to continue the download.
5. Click the RUN button to start the Download Manager.
   - Follow the instructions provided by the download management program.
6. The Computer will display a security warning asking you whether you want to continue with the download. Click the RUN button to continue.
   - The download management program will walk you through the entire download process.
   - A progress bar will appear showing you how the download process is going.
   - The computer will notify you when the downloading process is complete.

Chapter 9: Downloading & Installation!

Downloading a Program from the Internet: Visual Guide

Step 1:
Find the
program on the
Internet that
you would like
to download to
your computer.

Open the Adobe
website
www.adobe.com

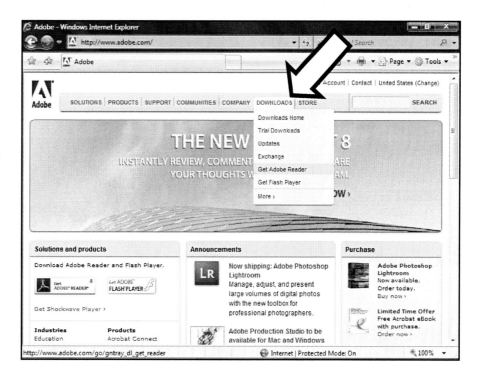

Click the
DOWNLOADS
link to display
the list of
available
programs.

Read the
program
description.

Step 2:
Click the
DOWNLOAD
ADOBE
READER link.

Chapter 9: Downloading & Installation!

Step 3:
The information bar and a warning message will appear to inform you a program is accessing your computer.

Step 3a:
Click the CLOSE button.

Step 3b:
Click on the Information Bar.

Step 3c:
Click the option
DOWNLOAD
FILE.

Step 4:
Choose the
option RUN.

Progress window
displays the rate
of the file
transfer.

Step 5:
Click the RUN
button to start
the Download
Management
program.

Progress window displays the progress of loading the program onto the computer.

Computer displays Security Warning.

Step 6:
Click the RUN button.

Click the NEXT button.

Click the INSTALL button.

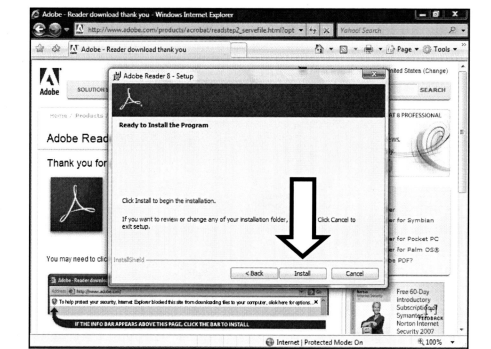

Progress window displays the computer's progress in loading the program.

Click the FINISH button.

Click the
ACCEPT button.

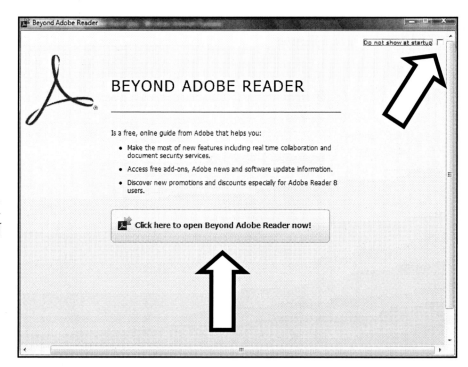

Click the
Checkbox "Do
not show at
startup."

Click the CLICK
HERE TO OPEN
BEYOND
ADOBE
READER NOW!
button.

The downloaded program has been successfully loaded onto the computer.

Close Adobe Reader.

Downloading a File from the Internet: Step by Step Instructions

1. Find the file on the Internet you would like to save to the computer.
2. Click the link for downloading the object. It should say something similar to DOWNLOAD or GET IT NOW.
3. The information bar and a warning message will appear to inform you a program is accessing your computer.
   a. Click the CLOSE button.
   b. Click on the Information Bar.
   c. Click the option DOWNLOAD FILE.
4. Click the option SAVE.
   • The Save As window will appear.
5. Tell the computer where you would like to save the program. Click the drop down arrow at the end of the "Save In:" box to choose a location. Choose DESKTOP from the list.
   • NOTE: Make certain you remember the file name and the location where the computer is saving the program.
6. Click the SAVE button.
   • A progress bar will appear showing you how the download process is going.
   • The computer will notify you when the downloading process is complete.

7. Once your download is complete, click the CLOSE button located in the download progress window.
8. Click the MINIMIZE button (-) to hide the Internet browser window.
   - The computer will display a new icon (picture) on the desktop for the newly downloaded program.

Downloading a File from the Internet: Visual Guide

Step 1:
Find the file on the Internet you would like to download to the computer.

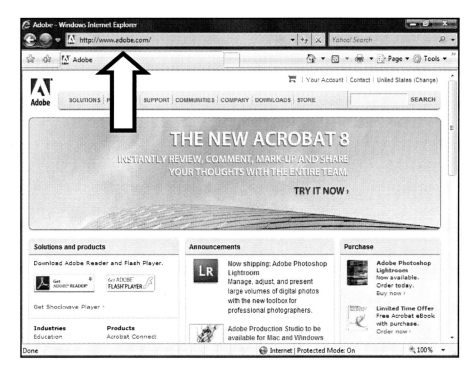

Open the Adobe website. www.adobe.com

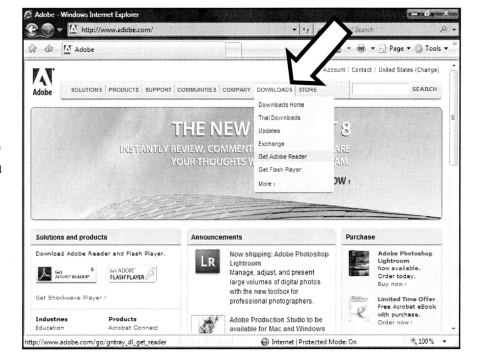

Click the DOWNLOADS link to display a list of available files.

Read the file description.

**Step 2:
Click the DOWNLOAD ADOBE READER link.**

**Step 3:
The information bar and a warning message will appear to inform you a program is accessing your computer.**

**Step 3a:
Click the CLOSE button.**

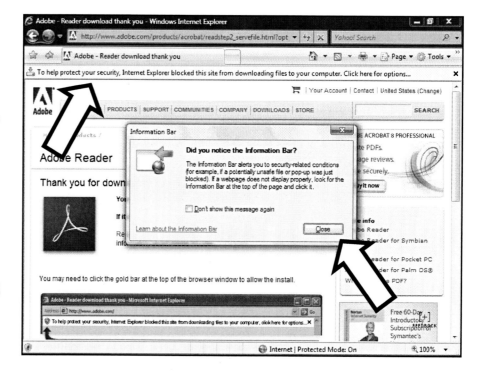

Chapter 9: Downloading & Installation!

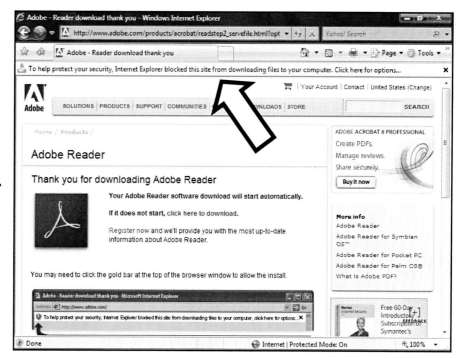

Step 3b:
Click on the
Information Bar.

Step 3c:
Click the option
DOWNLOAD
FILE.

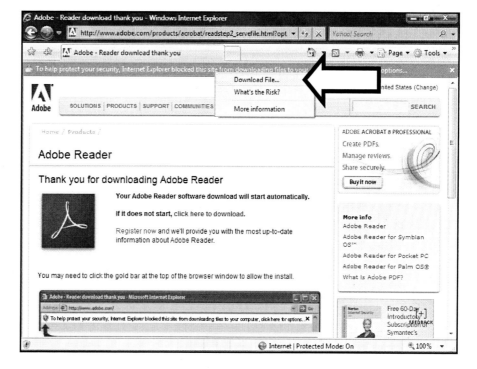

Step 4:
Click the SAVE
button.

The Save As
message box
will appear.

Step 5:
Click the drop down arrow at the end of the "Save In:" box to choose a location.
Choose DESKTOP from the list

Step 6:
Click the SAVE button.

Progress window displays the rate of the file transfer.

**Step 7:
Click the
CLOSE button.**

**Step 8:
Click the
MINIMIZE
button (-) to hide
the Internet
browser window**

Section 20:   Installation

Installing New Software

Anytime you want to add a new program to your computer, you have to install that program. Installation is the process of taking a new item (i.e. the downloaded program) and telling the computer how to use it.

There are two basic types of installations -- hardware and software. Installing hardware means adding a piece of equipment to your computer, such as a printer, fax, or scanner. Installing software means adding a program to your computer such as a game, word processing program, or instructions which tell your computer how to use a new piece of equipment.

Most programs are installed by compact disk (CD). If you go to the store and buy a new program for your computer, you will come home with a CD containing the program. The CD contains the information necessary for your computer to interact correctly with the new software. You can also get a program by downloading it from the Internet, as described in the previous section. Instead of using a CD to complete the installation process, you need to open the downloaded file (by double clicking on its icon). In the following example, you will install the program (Adobe Reader) you just downloaded to the computer.

The Installation Process

The installation process may vary depending upon what you are installing to your computer. These are general guidelines to help you get through the process.

WARNING: When installing software, make sure NO programs are running on the computer. You do not want any games or half written letters open on your computer. If you begin installing a program to your computer and you have other programs running at the same time, you may cause errors to occur in the installation process.

Chapter 9: Downloading & Installation!

Locate the file you just downloaded to your computer (Adobe Reader.) It should be on the computer's Desktop. Double-click the icon (picture) to open the file and begin the installation process. After you open the file, read and follow the directions which appear on the computer screen. In 90% of installations, the only thing you need to do is use your mouse to click on the OK or NEXT button. Generally the computer will tell you what to do. If you do not know what a particular screen is asking, do not worry. In most cases, the computer has already answered the question and is just asking you to confirm its choice. Simply click the OK or NEXT button.

The computer will tell you when it has finished installing the new program. When the installation process has finished, restart the computer unless the computer tells you differently.

HINT: During the Installation process, OK buttons perform the same function as NEXT buttons.

Installation Process: Step by Step Instructions
1. **Locate the program you want to install.**
   - **Put in the CD.**
   - **Find the icon of the downloaded program. Double-click on the icon to open the downloaded file.**
2. **Click the RUN button on the security screen.**
   - **The computer will begin to unpack the program files. It will also open the installation wizard (question screens). Be patient, the installation setup wizard will prompt you when it needs help.**
3. **Click the RUN button.**
4. **Click the NEXT button located on the introduction screen of the installation setup wizard.**
5. **The installation wizard will confirm that the new program is to be loaded on the computer. To verify this, click the INSTALL button.**
6. **Once Adobe Reader is installed, the setup box will say that it is complete. Click the FINISH button.**
   - **The computer will automatically run the newly installed program, but, in the future, you can open the program from the Start menu.**

Installation Process: Visual Guide

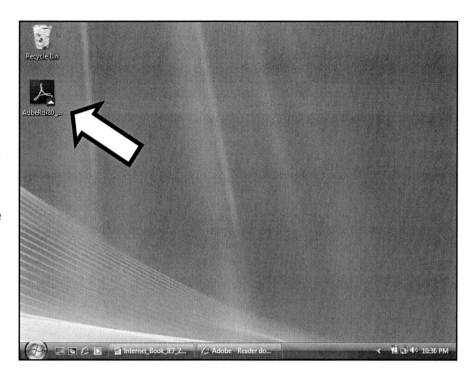

Step 1:
Locate the
downloaded file
on the desktop.

Double-click the
file's icon.

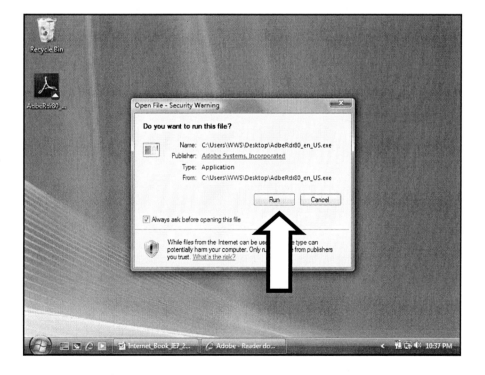

Step 2:
Click the RUN
button.

The computer will begin to unpack the program files. It will also open the installation wizard (question screens). Be patient, the installation setup wizard will prompt you when it needs help.

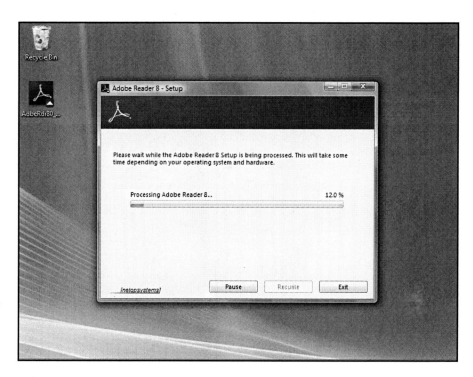

Step 3: Click the RUN button to continue the installation.

**Step 4:
Click the NEXT
button.**

**Step 5:
Click the
INSTALL
button.**

The computer will begin to load the files on the computer.

Step 6: Click the FINISH button.

The first time a new program is opened, the program will ask you to accept its license agreement. If you decline the agreement, the program will close and you will not be able to use it.

Click the ACCEPT button.

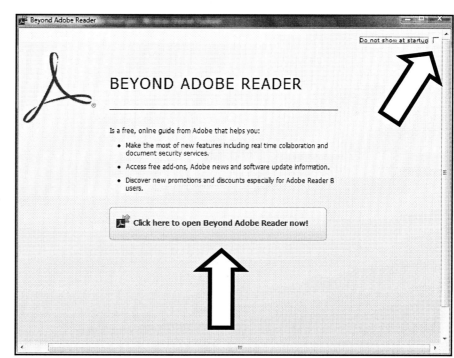

Click the Checkbox "Do not show at startup."

Click the CLICK HERE TO OPEN BEYOND ADOBE READER NOW! button.

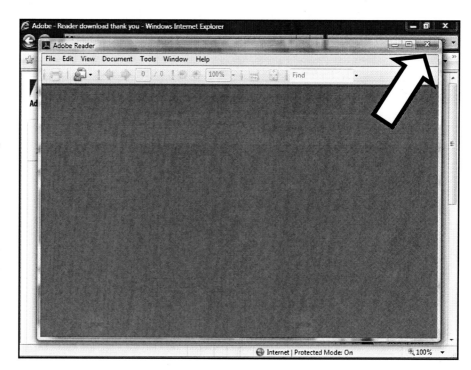

The downloaded program has been successfully loaded onto the computer.

Close Adobe Reader.

Section 21: Opening an Installed Program

Opening the Program

Once the program has been downloaded and installed, it is ready to use. The program can be accessed through either the Start menu or the Desktop icon. To open the program using the Desktop icon, position the mouse over the picture (icon) for the program and double-click the left mouse button. The program will open. The first time a program is opened, a license agreement will be displayed. If you accept the licensing agreement, you are promising that you will not resell the program or use it for illegal purposes. You have to accept the agreement to use the program. If you do not accept the agreement, the program will not work.

Open the Newly Installed Program: Step by Step Instructions

1. Locate the program's icon on the Desktop.
2. Double-click the icon to open the program.
   - A window will appear displaying the program's license agreement.
3. Click the ACCEPT button.

Open the Newly Installed Program: Visual Guide

Step 1:
Locate the program's icon on the Desktop.

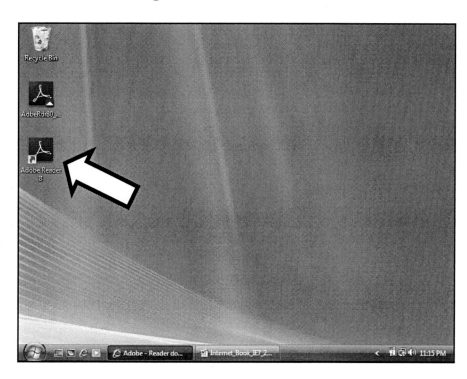

Step 2:
Double-click the icon to open program.

**Step 3:
Click the
ACCEPT button.**

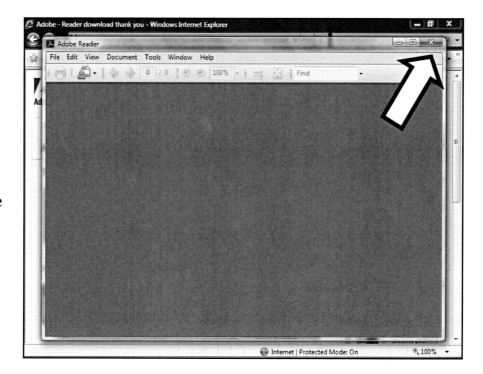

**The program
will open.**

**Click the Close
(X) button to
close the
window.**

Section 22: Removing a Desktop Icon

The installation process has completely saved all necessary information to the computer. Therefore, once the program has been installed, there is no need to keep the downloaded file. You can erase the file easily by using the click and drag method. Position the mouse pointer over the picture (icon) for the downloaded installation file (**not** the program icon). Click and hold down the left mouse button. The icon will turn blue. While holding down the mouse button, move the mouse over the recycle bin icon. Release the mouse button and the downloaded installation file will be moved into the trash.

Deleting a Desktop Icon: Step by Step Instructions

1. **Place the mouse arrow over the object you want to erase.**
2. **Click the left mouse button and hold it down.**
   - **While holding the left mouse button down, move your mouse arrow to the Recycle Bin.**
3. **When you arrive at the Recycle Bin, release the left mouse button. The icon will be placed in the trash.**
4. **Click the YES button on the warning message box.**

Deleting a Desktop Icon: Visual Guide

Step 1:
Place your
mouse arrow
over the object
that you want
to erase.

In this
example, you
will place your
mouse arrow
over the
installation
icon.

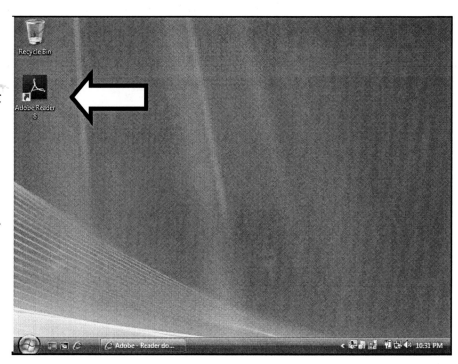

Step 2:
Click the left
mouse button
and hold it
down.

While holding
the left mouse
button down,
move your
mouse arrow to
the destination
(Recycle Bin).

The object will
follow.

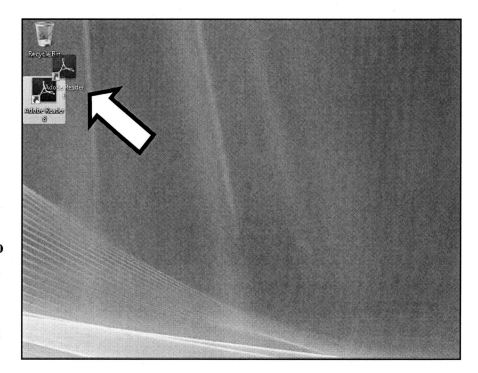

Step 3:
When you arrive at the Recycle Bin, release the left mouse button.

A warning message box will appear to ensure you want to delete the icon. Click the YES button.

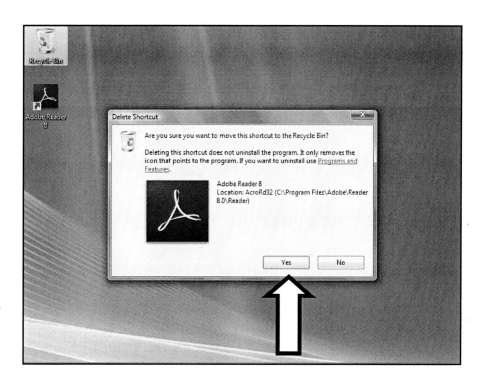

The object will be placed in the recycling bin.

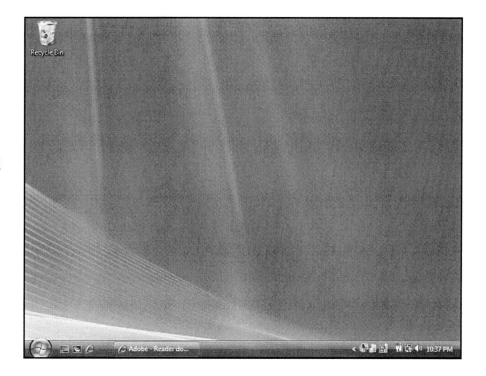

Section 23: Downloading RealPlayer®

RealPlayer

RealPlayer® is a music and video program for the computer. You can listen to music and watch videos right on your computer. The program is also very useful in transferring music to portable music players. RealPlayer® was created by RealNetworks and is available in two versions. Today, download the free player. If you later decide you would like more functionality, you can download the more advanced player.

The first thing you need to do is perform a specific search to locate the RealNetworks' website. Open the browser (you minimized the screen, so it should be located in your toolbar, at the bottom of your screen). Place your mouse pointer in the browser's address bar. Click the left mouse button once. Everything in the address bar will turn blue. Press the backspace button located on the keyboard. The web address will disappear. Now, type the address for the RealNetworks' website (www.real.com) in the address bar. When you are finished typing, press the Enter key on the keyboard. The computer will open the website.

Specific Search: Step by Step Instructions

1. **Position the mouse pointer over the input box located in the Address bar.**
2. **Click the left mouse button one time.**
3. **Press the Backspace key or the Delete key on the keyboard to erase the highlighted text.**
4. **Type the new website address in the input box.**
   - **Example: www.real.com**
5. **Press the Enter Key on your keyboard to go to the website.**

Specific Search: Visual Guide

Obtain a
website address.
(www.real.com)

Step 1:
Position the
mouse pointer
in the address
line.

Step 2:
Click the left
mouse button
one time.

Step 3:
Press the
Backspace key
or Delete key
on the
keyboard.

Step 4:
Type the new website address in the input box.

Step 5:
Press the Enter Key on your keyboard.

The Real Website.

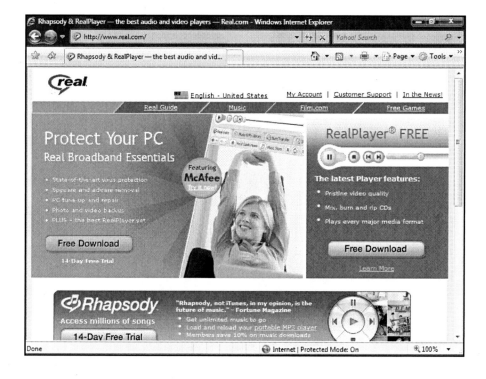

The next thing you need to do is find the item you wish to download from the website. Read the instructions to make sure you are downloading the correct program. In this example, make sure you are downloading the free RealPlayer® program, not the more advanced one.

After you have clicked the link to start the download, a window will appear asking you to begin downloading. Instead of saving the entire installation file to the computer, as you did in Adobe Reader, RealPlayer® will begin transferring the file immediately, as well as, beginning the installation process. Many people forget to erase the downloaded programs file once the program is installed. Since both processes are happening at once, you do not have to worry about it. This process also saves room on the computer. Select the RUN option and the process will begin. Be patient. Depending on the type of Internet connection you have, the download process may take a while to complete.

Downloading from the Internet: Step by Step Instructions
1. **Find the program on the Internet.**
2. **Click the link indicating a download is available.**
3. **Click the START REALPLAYER DOWNLOAD button.**
4. **Click the option RUN located on the message box to run the executable file to process the download.**

Downloading from the Internet: Visual Guide

**Step 1:
Find the
program on the
Internet.**

**Step 2:
Click the
FREE
DOWNLOAD
link.**

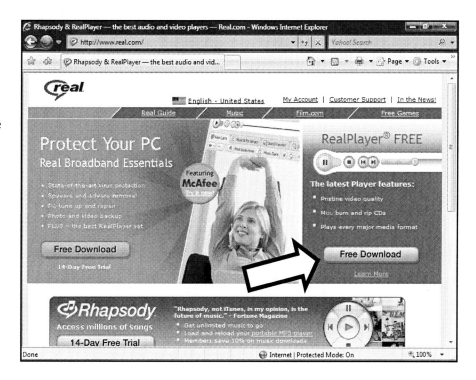

Scroll down and read the program description.

Step 2a:
Click the GET REALPLAYER FREE link.

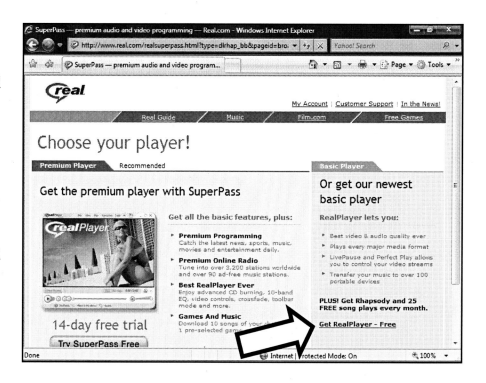

Scroll down to finish reading the download instructions.

Step 3:
Click the
START
REALPLAYER
DOWNLOAD
button.

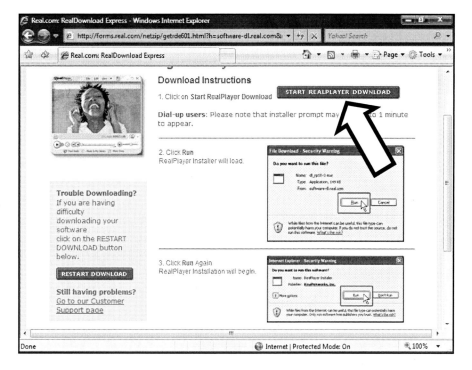

Step 4:
Click the RUN
button.

Be patient while the files download.

Once the download is complete, the installation process will begin.

The installation process has begun.

Section 24: Installing RealPlayer®

The creators of the RealPlayer® have instructed the computer to automatically begin the installation process after the files have finished downloading. At this point, your job is to read and follow the directions that appear on the computer screen. In 90% of installations, all you have to do is click on the OK or NEXT button(s) as the computer moves through the installation process. During this process, RealNetworks will instruct you to read their license agreement and accept the terms. Basically, you are agreeing to use the program yourself without selling it or breaking any laws. If you do not accept the agreement, you will not be able to use the program.

Installation Process: Step by Step Instructions

1. Click the ACCEPT button pertaining to the License Agreement.
2. The next screen inquires about your Internet connection. Select your Internet connection speed from the list provided. Dial-up is usually 56k.
3. Click the NEXT button.
4. Click the NEXT button.
5. Click the NEXT button.
6. Click the FINISH button.
   - The computer will automatically open the new program to finish the program setup.

Installation Process: Visual Guide

**Step 1:
Read the
License
Agreement.
Click the
ACCEPT
button.**

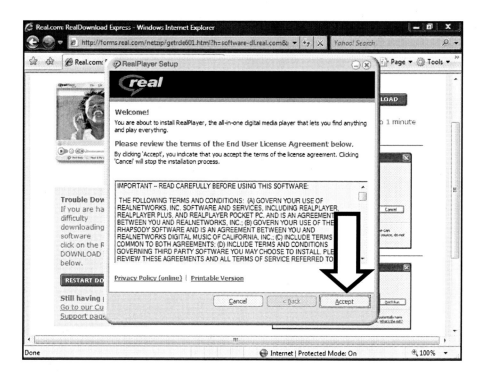

**Step 2:
Select your
Internet
connection
Speed from the
list provided.**

**Step 3:
Click the
NEXT button.**

Step 4:
Click the
NEXT button.

Further
instructions
will appear.

Step 5:
Click the
NEXT button.

Step 6:
Click the
FINISH
button.

To finish the setup, the program will connect to the company's computer system. After establishing a connection, the program will ask you if you want to load a new Google toolbar to the browser window. Decline the offer. Click the dot next to the option DO NOT INCLUDE THE GOOGLE TOOLBAR. Click the CONTINUE button.

The program creator, RealNetworks, will request information about the person who has downloaded the program. This information helps the company identify its user-base and provide better services in the future. Provide the requested information by typing in the input boxes provided. Remember to click the mouse in each box to activate it before typing. RealNetworks will also ask permission to contact you as new updates and products become available. You can refuse additional contact by clicking your mouse on the checkboxes located at the bottom of the web page. Each time you click a checkmark will disappear from its box. Click the CREATE button to move to the final step of the setup process.

The final step of the setup process is to confirm your desire to use the free version of the RealPlayer® program. Click the circle next to the option BASIC SETUP. A dot will appear in the circle. Click the CONTINUE button to finish the setup process. The RealPlayer® window will automatically open after the setup is complete.

Setup Process: Step by Step Instructions

1. Click the checkbox to the **DO NOT INCLUDE THE GOOGLE TOOLBAR** option. A dot will appear in the box.
2. Click the **NEXT** button.
   - The files will be copied to the computer's main memory
3. Click the **FINISH** button.
   - The installation program connects to the company's website in order to finish the setup process.
4. Click the circle next to the option **BASIC SETUP**. A dot will appear in the circle.
5. Click the **CONTINUE** button.
6. Type in the information requested in the input boxes provided.
7. Uncheck the boxes asking if you want to receive additional information. The checks will disappear.
8. Click the **CREATE** button.

Setup Process: Visual Guide

Step 1:
Click the checkbox next to the DO NOT INCLUDE THE GOOGLE TOOLBAR option.

Step 2:
Click the NEXT button.

The files will be copied to the computer's main memory.

Step 3: Click the FINISH BUTTON

The
installation
program
connects to the
company's
website to
finish the setup
process.

Step 4:
Click the circle
next to the
option BASIC
SETUP. A dot
will appear in
the circle.

Step 5:
Click the
CONTINUE
button.

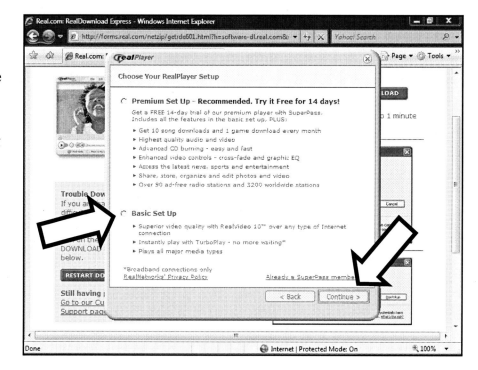

Step 6:
Type the requested information into the input boxes.

Step 7:
Uncheck the boxes asking if you want to receive additional information.

Step 8:
Click the CREATE button.

The installation program connects to the company's website to finish the setup process.

The setup process is complete.

Now that the program was successfully loaded onto the computer, you can go to the desktop of the computer and erase the extra desktop icons. Remove the unwanted icons from the desktop using the click and drag method.

Click the CLOSE (X) button to exit the RealPlayer® window.

Click the CLOSE (X) button to exit the browser window

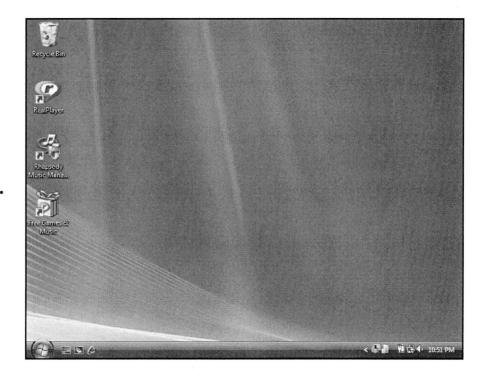

The new RealPlayer® icons are now on the Desktop.

Step 1:
Place your
mouse arrow
over the object
that you want
to erase.

Step 2:
Click the left
mouse button
and hold it
down.

While holding
the left mouse
button down,
move your
mouse arrow to
the destination
(the Recycle
Bin).

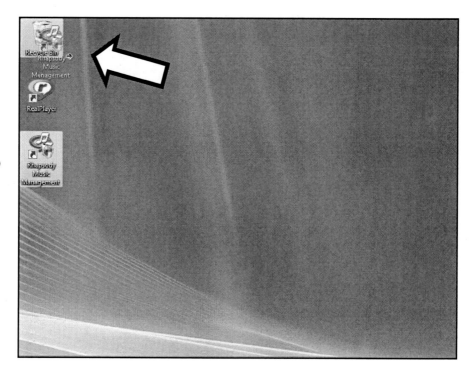

The object will
follow.

Step 3:
When you
arrive at the
Recycle Bin,
release the left
mouse button.

A warning
message box
will appear to
ensure you
want to delete
the icon. Click
the YES
button.

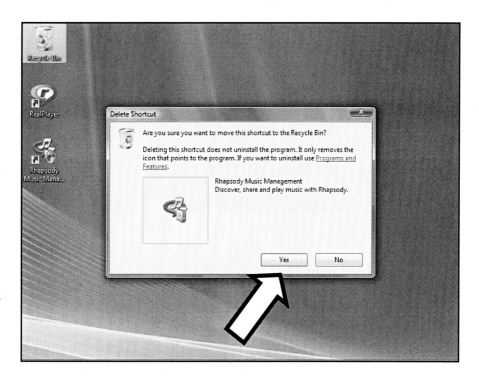

Repeat the
steps to erase
the remainder
of the icons.

The objects
will be placed
in the
Recycling Bin.

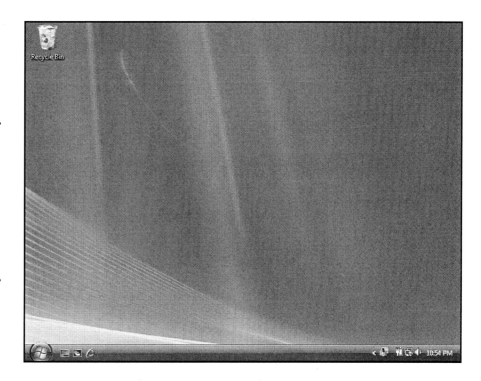

Chapter 9: Downloading & Installation!

Chapter 10

Advertising on the Internet!

What You Will Learn in this Chapter
- ✓ Advertising on the Internet
- ✓ Banner Ads
- ✓ Pop-up Ads
- ✓ Advertising Gimmicks
- ✓ Adware, Spyware, and Sneakware
- ✓ Protecting Yourself from Unethical Advertising Techniques

Section 25: Advertising on the Internet

Most of the information on the Internet is free to the public. This currently includes search engines, some online newspapers, news resources, e-mail, and instant messenger programs, just to name a few. Websites can afford to offer these items for free because the advertising revenue they generate takes the place of user paid fees.

Advertising is done through sponsored links, banner ads, and pop-up advertisements. The objective is to inform and draw people to websites related to a company or product. Sponsored links are often found on search engine result pages. The sponsored links take you directly to the advertiser's website. For example, both Google and Yahoo have sponsor links running down the right side of their results list. Banner ads are small pictures or video clips which appear on a web page. Banner ads are the most commonly used Internet advertising method. Click the left mouse button on a banner ad and the advertiser's website opens.

Do not be fooled by gimmicks - these ads are supposed to be enticing. For example, some ads say hit the target and win. The target will be moving quickly back and forth across the screen. Clicking on the ad (the target) will result in opening the company's website. These "contests" are just advertisements. Most advertisers pay the website owner every time someone clicks of their advertisement.

Many Internet users tend to ignore banner ads and sponsored links. So, to make sure their ads are being seen, some advertisers have implemented the use of pop-up advertisements. Pop-up ads open up in new windows, typically in front of the current browser window. These ads automatically open when a new web page is opened. Pop-up ads command your attention because you need to click on the ad's close (X) button to remove them. Advertisers like pop-up ads because they force Internet users to look and interact with the ads.

Internet advertisements are exactly like television commercials. They are annoying, but these ads keep the information on the Internet free for the public. Unfortunately, these ads have become an integral part of Internet experience.

Sponsor Link Advertising

Chapter 10: Advertising on the Internet!

Banner Advertising

Pop-up Ad Advertising

NOTE: Not all pop-up windows are advertising! Some website designers use pop-up windows to retrieve information or to direct you to a third party website.

Advertising Gimmicks

Some pop-up ads are very enticing. Here are a few tricks and catch phrases commonly used on pop-ups:

- You're a winner!
- Urgent – update your computer now!
- FREE!
- You have a message waiting for you!

If you received one of these advertisements in your mail box at home, you would probably throw the ad straight into the trash without ever opening the envelope. Treat on-line offers in the same manner.

A few advertisers even use deceptive ads to illicit customers. These advertisers design their ads to look like a Windows message box. The ads are still just links to their websites. You can use the mouse to decipher a real Windows message from an advertisement. Place the mouse pointer over a questionable item. If the mouse changes from a pointer into a hand, this is an indication that the box is an ad (a link to the company's website). If the mouse pointer remains an arrow, it is probably a real Windows message. Pay attention to the mouse pointer before you click!

Section 26: Internet Scams and Unwanted Advertising

What is Phishing?

Phishing is a scam that uses pop-up messages to deceive Internet users into disclosing credit card numbers, bank account information, social security numbers, passwords, or other sensitive information. The pop-up window/message might appear to be from a company you know and trust, but it is not. Most of these messages request urgent verification of your personal information. Con artists then collect your information instead of sending it to the real company. How do you know if a message is real or not? Well, when most legitimate institutions need information, they will call or send a letter. It is unlikely that they would use the Internet. If you suspect something may be a scam, call the company using a telephone number from the phone book or from a previous billing statement.

What is Adware?

Adware is unwanted advertising software that gathers information to track your Internet habits. Once your interests have been identified, the program then opens pop-up ads which deal with these activities. For example, you may be researching mortgage rates on-line, and within a short time, you begin receiving pop-up ads from mortgage companies from whom you have not requested information. You have been a casualty of Adware.

What is Spyware?

Spyware is a program that retrieves confidential information from your computer and then transmits it back to the organization that planted it on your computer. Spyware is typically installed without your knowledge and poses identity theft risks. One example of spyware is a keystroke logger. The program records all you've typed in an attempt to gather items including your social security number, credit card number, or bank account information.

What is Sneakware?

Sneakware is used to sneak onto your computer to make changes to your computer settings. Typical changes include changing your Home Page or adding a toolbar to the browser window. Unfortunately, sneakware is often attached to programs you download from the Internet. When you grant permission for the program to be installed, you may also be granting permission for a sneakware program. Read the License Agreements of all programs you download to ensure you know exactly what you are agreeing to.

Chapter 10: Advertising on the Internet!

Eliminating Adware, Spyware and Sneakware.

Many companies are coming to the aid of Internet users by creating programs to detect and remove these unwanted programs from the computer. Two popular programs used to combat this growing problem are Ad-aware by Lavasoft (www.lavasoftusa.com) and Search & Destroy by Spybot (www.safer-networking.org).

Each of these programs costs under $40, but each company also provides free trial versions of their programs. After the program is installed, scan your computer weekly. Remember to keep the software updated so it can detect the most recent evolutions of spyware, adware, and sneakware.

QUESTION: What is a trial version of a program?

ANSWER: A trial version of a program will run for a limited amount of time. This allows a computer user to try the software and see if you like it. If you do like the program, you will need to buy a more advanced version of the program after your trial period runs out. Remember, people created these programs to help protect your computer. You need to pay them for their time and effort. You do that by buying the program.

Chapter 10: Advertising on the Internet!

Chapter 11

Viruses!

What You Will Learn in this Chapter

- ✓ Viruses
- ✓ Spreading Viruses
- ✓ Internet Worms
- ✓ Protecting Yourself from Viruses and Worms
- ✓ Updating Windows
- ✓ Firewalls
- ✓ Starting Windows Firewall

Section 27: Viruses

What are Viruses?

Viruses are programs that you DO NOT want that are added to the computer without your knowledge or consent! Computer viruses range from small, unobtrusive files which are annoying to others that are malicious and destructive! A computer virus can affect the computer in many ways: viruses can erase programs or computer files, track Internet activity, collect personal data stored on the computer (i.e. passwords), slow down your Internet connection speed, or change the browser's Home Page. Just like a human virus, a computer virus's main objective is to reproduce and spread to other computers.

How do you get Viruses?

Viruses get into the computer in many different ways. The most frequent way viruses spread is via e-mail attachments. People unknowingly accept and send out e-mail messages with attachments that are infected with a computer virus. The computer file acts as the virus' host. When an infected e-mail attachment is opened, the virus is transferred to the computer. After the computer is infected, the virus will attempt to spread itself to other computers. Many viruses are designed to automatically send themselves to people in your e-mail address list. This just continues the cycle of infection.

Viruses have also been known to spread through Internet downloads. The virus will attach to a seemingly harmless program. When the program is downloaded, the virus is released onto the computer.

The last way viruses are spread is through infected files on a floppy disk or CD. When the files are opened, the virus is released.

Chapter 11: Viruses!

What is a Trojan Horse Virus?

A Trojan Horse is the term given to a destructive program that masquerades as a "good" application. For example, you could download a "free" screen-saver or music file which you intend to enjoy on the computer. What you do not know is that a virus is attached to the program. Remember the ancient city of Troy!

What are Worms?

A worm is a program that replicates itself over a computer network and usually performs malicious actions. A worm's most insidious characteristic is its ability to replicate and distribute itself to other computers. While viruses rely on attaching to another program, worms can replicate independently. They hide in a computer and create copies of themselves. The result can be a simple display in a text message, warning you of the intrusion, or in the worst cases, all the files on your hard drive will be renamed, overwritten, or erased! For example, the "ILOVEYOU" worm spread by sending itself to all e-mail contacts in the person's e-mail address book, repeatedly, and at scheduled intervals. This worm disabled some company computer systems until a fix was developed.

Virus Protection

An anti-virus program, such as Symantec's Norton AntiVirus or McAfee AntiVirus, is the first line of defense against viruses and worms. The anti-virus software scans your computer files regularly, looking for unusual changes in file size, programs that match the program's database of known viruses, suspicious e-mail attachments, and other warning signs. Keep your antivirus software running at all times and update it often because new viruses come out daily.

The second line of defense against infection is common sense. First, do not open e-mail from an unknown source. Delete it immediately. You never know what someone is sending you, especially if you do not know the sender. Second, if you get an e-mail containing an attachment that seems out of the ordinary, delete the whole message. Remember, some viruses spread using e-mail addresses stored in e-mail address books. If something looks strange, delete the message and then ask the person who sent the message if they sent it. If it was important, ask them to send it to you again. Third, do not download programs or files from a website unless you know and trust the source.

Chapter 11: Viruses!

Keeping these ideas in mind will help protect you, your computer, and the files saved on it. Treat websites with the same common sense and caution you would show to any other stranger asking you for money or personal information, or offering a get rich quick "opportunity." If it looks too good to be true, it probably is.

Keep your computer software up to date. Updates will block many of the security holes used by worms and viruses. Microsoft provides security patches for its programs including Windows, Outlook, and Internet Explorer. As problems are discovered in software, the creator provides fixes and new security patches.   These updates are free and help keep your computer and information safe.

QUESTION: How do I check to see if there are updates available for my programs?

ANSWER: Microsoft provides all updates through its website. To check for updates, open the "All Programs" list available through the Start menu. Within the All Programs menu you will find the Windows Update option. The Windows Update option will connect your computer to Microsoft's website and check for updates. If updates are available, you will have the choice to update the computer.

Depending on how many updates need to be downloaded and installed, the update process may take a large amount of time to complete. Once the computer has started, it will do all the work. Microsoft recommends checking for new updates on a daily basis. Perform the update at a time when you can leave your computer connected to the Internet. Before the updates download, the computer will generate an approximate time limit for the updating process. If multiple updates are recommended, consider downloading them one at a time to shorten the process.

Updating Windows: Step by Step Instructions

1. Open the START menu.
2. Click ALL PROGRAMS.
3. Click the WINDOWS UPDATE option or do a specific search for
   http://windowsupdate.microsoft.com using the address bar of your
   Internet browser.

Updating Windows: Visual Guide

Step 1:
Open the
START Menu.

STEP 2:
CLICK ALL
PROGRAMS

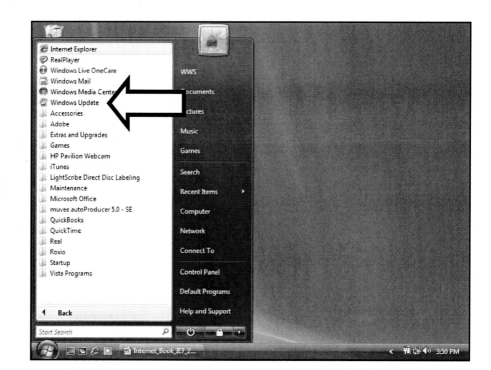

**Step 3:
Click the
WINDOWS
UPDATE
option.**

Section 28:   Firewalls

A firewall is a system designed to protect a computer or network of computers from unauthorized access. In principle, think of a firewall as two security guards at a country club. One guard is there to prevent people from trespassing on the private property, and the other is there to let authorized people enter. A firewall does both jobs. Unfortunately, there are people in the world that like to steal and destroy others' property. The firewall's job is to protect you from these people, while still enabling you to get your work done. To help protect your home computer, turn on the firewall built into Windows XP.

Turning on Windows Firewall: Step by Step Instructions

1. Open the START menu.
2. Click the CONTROL PANEL option.
3. Click the SECURITY option.
4. Click the TURN WINDOWS FIREWALL ON OR OFF option.
5. Click the CHANGE SETTINGS option
   - If a warning screen appears indicating the computer needs permission to make a change to the setting, click the CONTINUE button.
6. Click the ON (recommended) option.
7. For added security click the BLOCK ALL INCOMING CONNECTIONS checkbox.
   - Used for maximum protection, such as when a dangerous virus or worm is spreading over the Internet.
8. Click the OK button.

Turning on Windows Firewall: Visual Guide

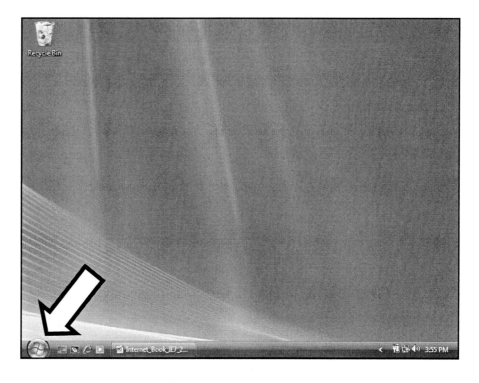

Step 1:
Open the
START Menu.

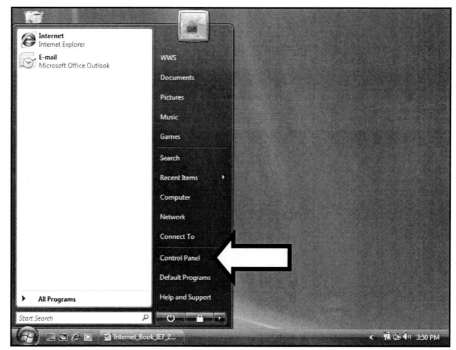

**Step 2:
Click the
CONTROL
PANEL option.**

**Step 3:
Click the
SECURITY
option.**

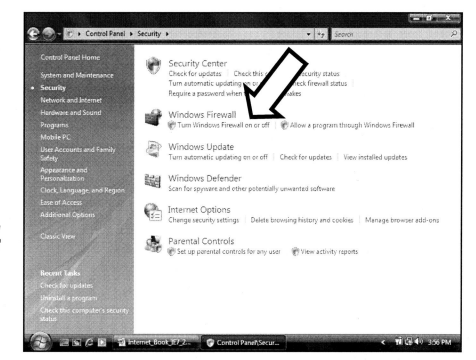

Step 4:
Click the
TURN
WINDOWS
FIREWALL
ON OR OFF
option.

Step 5:
Click the
CHANGE
SETTINGS
option.

If a warning
screen appears,
click the
CONTINUE
button.

Step 6:
Click the ON"
option.

Step 7:
For added
security click the
BLOCK ALL
INCOMING
CONNECTIONS
checkbox.

Step 8:
Click the OK
button.

If you have Windows 2000 or an earlier version, your computer probably does not have a firewall. You can install firewalls purchased from a third party vendor. Two firewalls for home use are Norton Personal Firewall (www.symantec.com) and ZoneAlarm (www.zonelabs.com). Each of these programs is under $50 and designed for a home computer.

With all of these potential hazards, it begins to feel like the Internet is a hostile and dangerous place and should be totally avoided. But the good news is, if you take certain precautions and use common sense, you can enjoy the Internet and its resources without worry.

Chapter 12

Printing from the Internet!

What You Will Learn in this Chapter
- ✓ The Printing Process
- ✓ Previewing a Page Before Printing
- ✓ Printing only Part of a Page

Section 29: Printing

The Printing Process

You can print a paper copy of information you find on the Internet if you have a printer connected to your computer. To print, you need to open the Print menu. The Print menu can be accessed using the black down arrow immediately to the right of the Print button on the browser command bar. Click your left mouse button on the down arrow and the print menu will open. Slide your mouse arrow down the Print menu and click on the option "Print." The menu will close and a Print screen will appear.

There are several important features on the print screen. At the top, you will see the name of your printer. On the left side of the screen is the page range. Page range shows you how many document pages will be printed. Remember, web pages are like Egyptian scrolls. One web page may take multiple pieces of paper to print. For example, a web page may look like only one page, but might use three pieces of paper when printed on 8x11 sheets of paper. Page range refers to the number of physical pages required to print the web page. For example, you can choose to print all of the web page's information or only a specific page (e.g. Page 1 equals the first page or top of the web page). The computer is set to automatically use the "ALL" option, meaning it will print the entire web page, regardless of the physical number of pieces of paper it will take.

If you do not want to print every page of your document, you have two options. You can choose to print only a selection of text or only specific pages of text. To print a selection of text, you must first highlight (turn blue) the section you desire. This option is very handy when you want to conserve ink and only need to print specific sections of a web page.

Chapter 12: Printing from the Internet!

The second option, PAGES, permits you to type in the specific page number(s) of the page(s) to be printed. For example, if you only want to print the top of the web page, you can type "1" in the page number box. Only one physical piece of paper will be printed. If you want to print pages 1, 3, and 5, type 1,3,5 in the input box. If you want to print pages 1 through 5, type 1-5 in the box.

The right side of the print screen contains the option "Number of Copies." This allows you to choose the number of times you want the computer to print the selected document or file. The computer has been programmed to print one copy. If you need more than one copy, you must change this option by clicking on the tiny up and down arrows located on the right side of the small white input box located to the right of the heading "Number of Copies." Each click of the tiny up and down arrows will change the number in the white input box.

Located just below the "Number of Copies" heading is another option called "Collate." The Collate option can be either checked (turned on) OR unchecked (turned off). The Collate option is only used if you are printing multiple copies of a web page. When collate is checked, the computer will print one full copy of the web page, then print the next full copy, and so on, with all pages in the proper sequence. If the Collate option is unchecked (off), the computer will print all the copies of page one, then all the copies of page two, then all the copies of page three, and so on. You will then have to put the copies in order manually. As you can see, making certain the Collate option is checked can save you a lot of time and effort.

After you choose the number of copies and the page range you want, click on the PRINT button located on the lower right side of the print screen. The print screen will close, and your printer will make a paper copy of the web page.

Example Print screen.

Page Range Section on left.

Number of Copies on right.

PRINT button bottom center.

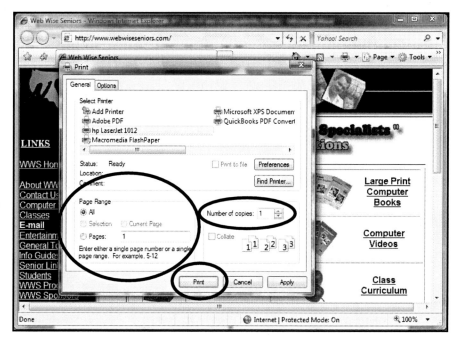

Printing a File (One Copy): Step by Step Instructions

1. Click on the DOWN ARROW next to the Print button on the command bar.
2. Click the PRINT option.
3. Choose the Page Range and Number of Copies desired.
4. Click the PRINT button.

Printing a File (One Copy): Visual Guide

Step 1:
Click on the DOWN ARROW next to the Print button on the command bar.

Step 2:
Click on the PRINT option.

Chapter 12: Printing from the Internet!

Step 3:
Choose the Page
Range and
Number of
Copies desired.

Step 4:
Click the
PRINT button.

NOTE: The Print button located on the command bar will automatically print the entire web page without opening the print window. To use the options found on the print screen, open the print screen by using the down arrow to the right of the Print option located on the command bar.

Printing a File (Multiple Copies): Step by Step Instructions

1. Click on the DOWN ARROW next to the Print button on the command bar.
2. Click the PRINT option.
3. (Optional): Select "Page Range" and "Number of Copies"
4. Make certain the COLLATE option has a checkmark next to it.
5. Click on the PRINT button.

Printing a File (Multiple Copies): Visual Guide

Step 1:
Click on the
DOWN
ARROW next
to the Print
button on the
command bar.

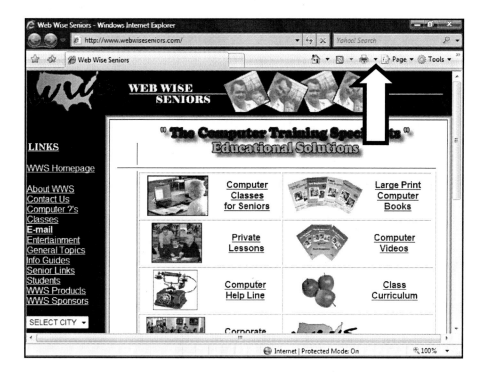

Step 2:
Click on the
PRINT option.

Step 3:
Select "Page Range" and "Number of Copies"

Step 4:
Make certain the COLLATE option has a check mark next to it.

Step 5:
Click on the PRINT button.

Section 30: Print Preview

The Print Preview Option

Another helpful feature available through the Internet browser is Print Preview, which is the ability to see what a web page will look like once it has been printed. The Print Preview option is located in the Print menu. Clicking PRINT PREVIEW will display a new screen showing you a zoomed out perspective of the printed page. It will enable you to see the entire page, including margins. The image displayed in this screen is exactly what will be printed out.

Located at the top of the Print Preview screen is a helpful toolbar which enables you to change how you view the previewed document. This toolbar contains options giving you the ability to zoom in and out, view multiple pages at once, and more. When you have finished looking at the preview screen, click on the red "X" in the upper right corner of the window.

Opening Print Preview: Step by Step Instructions

1. **Click on the DOWN ARROW to the right of the Print button on the command bar.**
2. **Click on PRINT PREVIEW option.**

Opening Print Preview: Visual Guide

Step 1:
Click on the DOWN ARROW next to the Print button on the command bar.

**Step 2:
Click the
PRINT
PREVIW
option.**

**Example of
Print Preview
Mode**

**The Toolbar
enables you to
change views
and print the
page.**

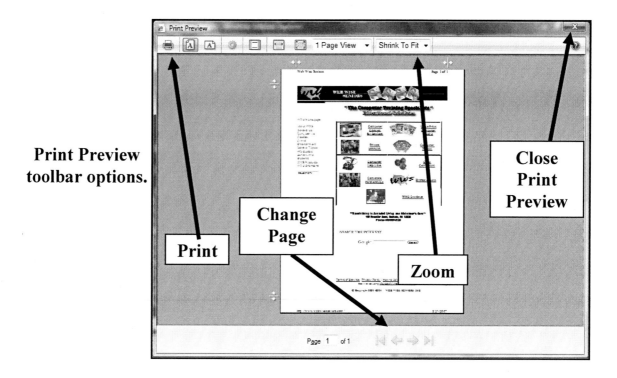

Print Preview toolbar options.

Close Print Preview

Change Page

Print

Zoom

Section 31: Printing Only Part of a Page

The Print Selection Option

Printing web pages can be very costly and produce a lot of waste. Many times you only need one paragraph or a small section of a web page, but, when you print the page, the entire page prints including the section you desire. To conserve paper and money, try highlighting a section of the web page and using the SELECTION option found on the print screen. Highlight the section you want to print. The Print menu can be accessed using the black down arrow immediately to the right of the Print button on the browser command bar. Click your left mouse button on the down arrow and the print menu will open. Slide your mouse arrow down the Print menu and click on the option "Print." The Selection option is located under the page range heading. The Selection option will only be available if part of the web page is highlighted before opening the print screen.

Chapter 12: Printing from the Internet!

Highlighting

Highlighting is used to tell the computer what specific part of the web page you want. Once a selection of text is highlighted, it may be copied or printed. To highlight text, position your mouse arrow at the end of the text you want to select. Click and HOLD DOWN the left mouse button. While holding down the mouse button, move your mouse arrow to the beginning of the text you want to select. As the mouse moves over the text, it will turn blue or black. This is called being highlighted. After reaching the beginning of the desired text, release the mouse button. The selected text will remain highlighted until you click in the display area again. The computer is now ready to work with your selected text.

When you highlight text, the computer is only concerned about the data between where you began holding down the left mouse button and the exact point at which you released the left mouse button. Think of these positions as two dots. Anything between these dots will be highlighted. How you move from one location to another (left to right, or right to left) does not matter. The computer only focuses on the area between those two dots.

For this example, open the "About WWS" page located on the Web Wise Seniors' website (www.webwiseseniors.com). The link to "About WWS" is located on the left side of the Web Wise Seniors Home Page. Once the page is displayed, try to highlight the first paragraph. Position the mouse after the period at the end of the first paragraph. Click and hold down the left mouse button. Move your mouse across the text until it is positioned before the first word in the paragraph. The entire paragraph should be highlighted. Release your mouse button.

WARNING: Don't release the left mouse button until the entire paragraph has been highlighted. Releasing the button will stop the highlighting process before you have included all the text. If you do release the mouse button, you have to start the highlighting process over again.

The only thing more important than knowing how to highlight text, is knowing how to un-highlight text. If you accidentally highlight an area, click your mouse anywhere in the display area one time. A single click will remove all the highlighting on the page.

Highlighting Your Text: Step by Step Instructions

1. Position the mouse at the end of the desired text.
2. Click and hold down the left mouse button.
3. Move the mouse to the beginning of the desired text.
4. Release the mouse button.
   - The dark background indicates it has been highlighted.

Highlighting Your Text: Visual Guide

Open the Web Wise Seniors web page.

www. webwiseseniors .com

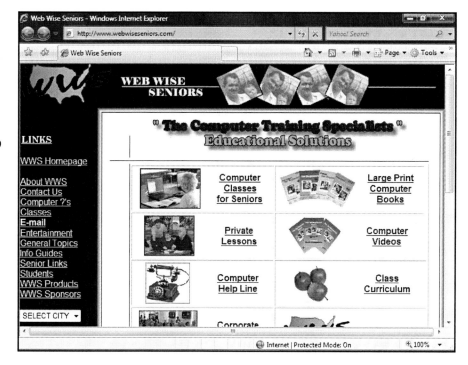

Click on the "About WWS" link.

Step 1: Position the mouse at the end of the desired text.

Step 2: Click and hold down the left mouse button.

Step 3:
Move the mouse
to the beginning
of the desired
text.

Step 4:
Release the
mouse button.

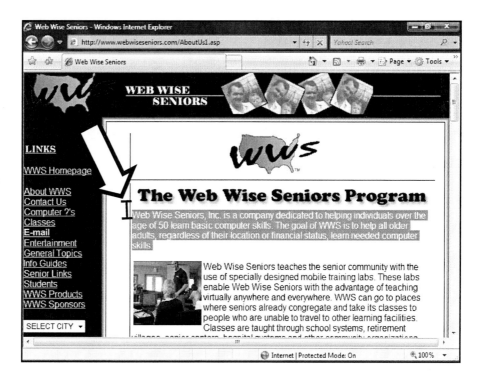

Chapter 12: Printing from the Internet!

Printing a Selection: Step by Step Instructions

1. Click on the DOWN ARROW to the right of the Print button on the command bar.
2. Click the PRINT option.
3. Click the SELECTION option located under the Page Range heading.
4. Click the PRINT button.

Printing a Selection: Visual Guide

Step 1:
Click the
DOWN
ARROW to the
right of the
Print button on
the command
bar.

Step 2:
Click the
PRINT option.

Step 3:
Click the
SELECTION
option located
under the Page
Range heading.

Step 4:
Click the
PRINT button.

Un-highlight the text.

Click the mouse anywhere in the display window.

The text has been successfully un-highlighted.

Chapter 13

Saving from the Internet!

What You Will Learn in this Chapter
- ✓ Saving an Internet Web Page
- ✓ Saving a Picture from the Internet
- ✓ Saving Text from the Internet

While searching the Internet, you may find data or images you would like to save for future use. Remember, data and images found on an Internet website are the property of the creator. Even though the computer will allow you to copy almost anything off a website, be careful about how you use the item. Legally you do not own it. You can use the item for personal use, but it is illegal (plagiarism) to professionally use or sell another person's work unless you have permission.

Section 32: Saving Items from the Internet

What Does the Term "Saving" Mean?

When you are using the Internet, each web page is stored in the computer's temporary memory while it is displayed by the browser. When the computer is shut off, the temporary memory is erased. This means, if you want to see the information on the web page again, you have to return to the website. When you save something, the item is usually stored in your computer's main memory. Saving enables you to the view the item at a later time, on or off the Internet, without loss of information.

The saving process itself is not difficult. The hard part is remembering where you saved the files and what you named them, so you can find them easily in the future. Internet Explorer is set up to store all your text in a folder titled Documents and all images in a folder titled My Pictures. These folders are located on the computer's main memory, which is usually referred to as the Local Disk, C: drive, or hard drive. In the next few examples, you are going to save an entire web page, as well as a picture located on a web page.

Chapter 13: Saving from the Internet!

Saving a Web Page

Most people do not save websites to the computer. Most important websites are added to the Favorites list. This provides access to the page from its original location. When the site is opened from the Favorites list, any changes made by the web page designer will be shown. Saving the page to your computer takes a snapshot of the page and saves it to the computer's main memory. The snapshot remembers the information exactly as you viewed it.

To save a web page, display it in the browser window. For this example, open the "Classes" page located on the Web Wise Seniors' website (www.webwiseseniors.com). The link to "Classes" is located on the left side of the Web Wise Seniors Home Page. Once the page is displayed, you can begin the save process. Position the mouse arrow on the PAGE button located on the browser command bar. Click the left mouse button once to open the PAGE menu. Move the mouse arrow down to the SAVE AS option and click the left mouse button. This closes the PAGE menu and opens the save screen. There are three additional steps to complete the save process. First, you must choose where to save the file. Second, you have to give the file a name and, third, you must click the SAVE button.

First, you need to tell the computer where you want to save the file. At the top of the save screen is the heading SAVE IN: followed by a white box and a gray arrow pointing down. This gray arrow tells you that the box is a drop down menu. If you click on the gray arrow, a list will appear displaying the locations where you can save your file. If the white box currently displays DESKTOP, you are in the right location. If it does not display DESKTOP, you need to choose DESKTOP from the list.

To change the location to DESKTOP, place your mouse arrow on the gray drop down arrow and click your left mouse button. Position the mouse arrow over the DESKTOP option from the drop down list that appears. It will turn blue. To make the selection, click the left mouse button. The list will close, and DESKTOP will be displayed in the "Save In" box. You have now finished the first part of the save process.

Chapter 13: Saving from the Internet!

The second step is to choose a name for the file. Located near the bottom of the save screen you will see the heading "FILE NAME." To the right of the heading "FILE NAME" will be a white input box containing a web page name. The name in the input box is the computer's suggestion for a name. For this example, keep the name provided by the computer and move on to the third step of the save process.

NOTE: To change the suggested name, move your mouse arrow to the end of the name and click the left mouse button. Clicking the mouse activates the box and drops the cursor (blinking line) at the location the mouse was clicked. Use the backspace key on the keyboard to erase the suggested name. When the name has been erased, type in the desired name using the keyboard.

NOTE: When choosing a name, you can use up to 256 characters. The file name may include any numbers (0-9) and letters (A-Z), but not colons, semicolons, slashes, or mathematical operators (for example, the plus and minus signs). It is recommended that you use a maximum of three or four short words. If the name is too long, you will not see the full name when it is displayed in lists. By keeping it short, you have a better chance of seeing the entire name displayed when searching through the computer. This will help you later when you are looking for your work. If the name is too long, the computer will only show part of the name followed by three dots.

The final step in the saving process is to click the SAVE button located on the bottom right side of the save screen. When you click the SAVE button, the computer will close the save screen, and the file will be successfully saved to the computer's main memory.

Chapter 13: Saving from the Internet!

QUESTION: How do you know the web page was saved successfully?

ANSWER: If you minimize the browser window, you will see a new icon located on the Desktop. This verifies the page was saved correctly.

Locate the Example Web Page: Step by Step Instructions
1. Open the Web Wise Seniors website by doing a specific search using the website address: www.webwiseseniors.com
2. Click the link "Classes" located on the left side of the WWS page.

Saving a Web Page: Step by Step Instructions
1. Click on the PAGE button located on the command bar.
2. Click the SAVE AS option.
3. Locate the SAVE IN box, and click the black arrow to open the drop down list.
4. Click the option DESKTOP.
5. Locate the FILE NAME box and view the name of page.
6. Click the SAVE button.

Saving a Web Page: Visual Guide

Step 1:
Open the website address www. webwiseseniors .com

Step 2:
Click the link CLASSES.

Begin the Save Process

Step 1:
Click on the PAGE button.

Step 2:
Click the SAVE
AS option.

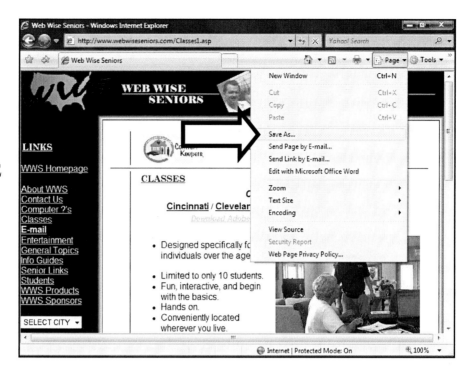

Step 3:
Locate the
SAVE IN box,
and click the
black arrow to
open the drop
down list.

Step 4:
Click the option
DESKTOP.

Step 5:
Locate the FILE
NAME box and
view the name
of the page.

Step 6:
Click the SAVE
button.

Verify the web page was saved successfully.

Click the Minimize button to view the Desktop.

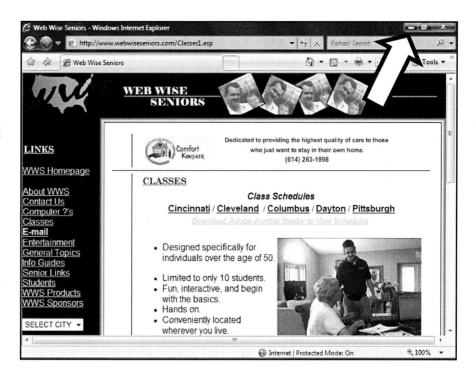

Locate the icon for the saved web page.

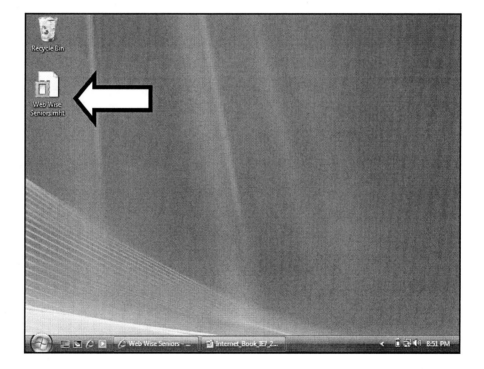

Chapter 13: Saving from the Internet!

Saving Pictures from the Internet

Often while browsing the Internet, you will find a picture you would like to save. Most images located on the Internet can be saved, but remember these images are the property of the creator. Typically, if you do not commercially reproduce or attempt to sell the image, you will not have any problems.

For this example, go to the Web Wise Seniors "Classes" page and view the first image. Try to scroll the page to view a large portion of the total picture. Position the mouse over the image and click the right mouse button. A shortcut menu will appear. Place your mouse over the SAVE PICTURE AS option and click the left mouse button. The Save screen will open. There are three additional steps to complete the save process. First, you must choose where to save the file. Second, you have to give the file a name and, third, you must click the SAVE button.

If you are continuing from the last example (where we saved the web page) the browser window is already open, but currently minimized. Locate the browser button in the blue task bar located at the bottom of the Desktop. Click the button that contains either the name of the browser or the name of the current web page in it. The browser window will redisplay.

If you closed your browser, open the browser using the Start menu and do a specific search for www.webwiseseniors.com.

Locate the Example Web Page: Step by Step Instructions
1. **Open the Web Wise Seniors website by doing a specific search using the website address (www.webwiseseniors.com).**
2. **Click the CLASSES link located on the left side of the WWS page.**

Saving Pictures: Step by Step Instructions

1. Find an image on the Internet.
2. Position the mouse over the image and click the right mouse button. A shortcut menu will appear.
3. Click the SAVE PICTURE AS option from the list provided. The save screen will appear.
4. Locate the SAVE IN box. The SAVE IN box should display the name "Pictures."
5. Locate the FILE NAME box and view the name of picture. Either leave the currently displayed name in the box or type a new name.
6. Click the SAVE button.

Saving Pictures: Visual Guide

Open the website address. www. webwiseseniors .com

Click the CLASSES link.

Step 1:
Locate the
desired image.

Step 2:
Position the
mouse over the
image and click
the right mouse
button. A
shortcut menu
will appear.

Step 3:
Click the SAVE
PICTURE AS
option.

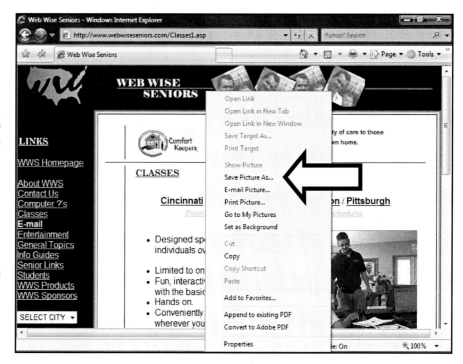

Chapter 13: Saving from the Internet!

Step 4:
Locate the SAVE IN box. The SAVE IN box should display the name "Pictures."

Step 5:
Locate the FILE NAME box and view the name of picture.

Chapter 13: Saving from the Internet!

If you want to, rename the picture:

Click at the end of the current name.

Press the Backspace key on the keyboard.

Type a new name for the picture.

**Step 6:
Click the SAVE
button.**

**The image has
been saved to
the computer's
main memory.**

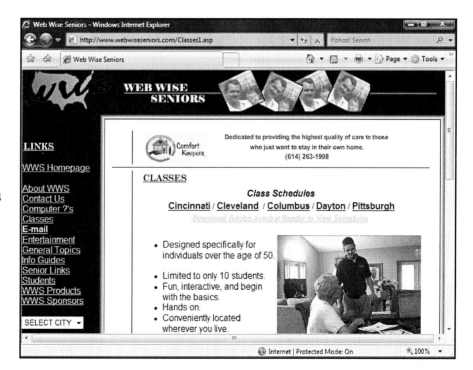

Once pictures have been saved, take a moment to verify they have been saved correctly. The pictures were saved into the Pictures folder of the computer's hard drive. Access the Pictures folder using the Start Menu.

Verifying the Pictures are Saved: Step by Step Instructions

1. Open the START Menu by clicking the START button.
2. Click the PICTURES option.
3. Locate the image name in the list provided.
4. Double-click on the icon representing the image listing. The picture should appear on your computer screen.
5. Click the CLOSE (X) button to exit the image.
6. Click the CLOSE (X) button to exit the Pictures window.

Verifying the Pictures are Saved: Visual Guide

**Step 1:
Click the
START button.**

**Step 2:
Click the
PICTURES
option.**

**Step 3:
Locate the
image name in
the list
provided.**

**Step 4:
Double-click on
the icon
representing
the image
listing.**

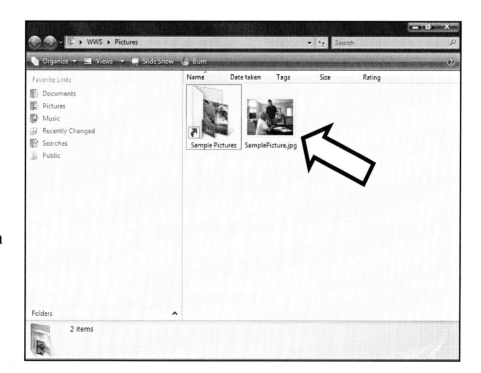

The picture will appear on your screen.

Step 5:
Click the CLOSE (X) button to exit the image.

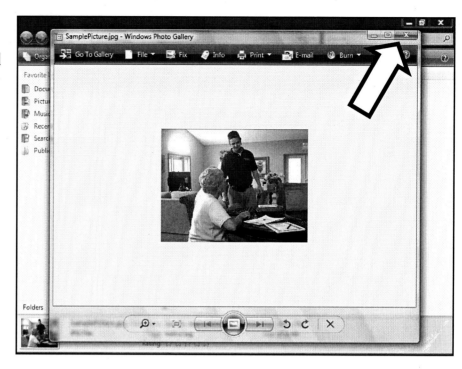

Step 6:
Click the CLOSE (X) button to close the PICTURES window.

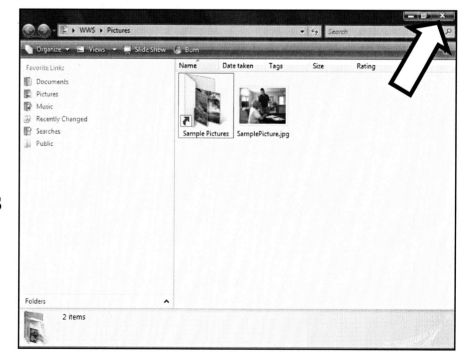

Chapter 13: Saving from the Internet!

Saving Text from the Internet

The next example will explain how to select a piece of text from a web page and save it. The process will use the concepts of highlighting, copying and pasting, and saving. Being able to save text from a web page without saving the whole page is a very useful tool.

Go back to the Web Wise Seniors Home Page. Then click on the ABOUT WWS link located on the left side of the page. Locate and highlight the first two paragraphs. Once the text is highlighted, use the PAGE button on the command bar to copy the text. After the text is copied, open a word processing program (e.g. Microsoft Word) and Paste the copied text into the new word processing document. Once the text has been pasted into the new document, save the document to the DOCUMENTS folder located on the computer's hard drive (main memory).

Open the browser screen and do a specific search for the Web Wise Seniors Home Page (www.webwiseseniors.com). Locate the address bar at the top of your browser window. Move your mouse pointer over any part of the white input box and click the left mouse button one time. Everything in the input box will turn blue. Use the Backspace key or the Delete key on the keyboard to erase the highlighted text. Begin typing the new website address (i.e. www.webwiseseniors.com). When you are finished typing, either hit the Enter key on your keyboard. The web page will open. Then click on the ABOUT WWS link on the left side of the page.

Specific Search: Step by Step Instructions
1. Obtain a website address.
2. Position the mouse pointer over the input box located in the address line.
3. Click the left mouse button one time.
4. Press the Backspace key or the Delete key on the keyboard to erase the highlighted text.
5. Type the new website address in the input box.
   - Remember a website address typically includes:
     o www. followed by
     o The unique name, followed by
     o The ending (.com, .gov, .net, .org, .edu or .cc)
       ▪ Example: www.WebWiseSeniors.com
6. Press the Enter key on the keyboard to go to the website.

Specific Search: Visual Guide

Step 1:
Obtain a
website address.

Step 2:
Position the
mouse pointer
over the input
box located in
the address line.

Step 3:
Click the left
mouse button
once.

Step 4:
Press the
Backspace or
Delete Key to
erase the name.

Step 5:
Type the new
website address
in the input
box.

Step 6:
Press the Enter
key on the
keyboard to go
to the website.

Chapter 13: Saving from the Internet!

The Web Wise Seniors' Home Page.

The Web Wise Seniors' ABOUT WWS page.

The next step is to highlight the first two paragraphs on the Web Wise Seniors' About WWS Page.

Highlighting

Highlighting tells the computer you want to work with that particular part of the web page. To highlight text, position your mouse arrow at the end of the text you want to select. Click and HOLD DOWN the left mouse button. While holding down the mouse button, move your mouse arrow to the beginning of the selection. As the mouse moves over the text, it becomes highlighted (will have a black/blue background). After reaching the beginning of the desired text, release the mouse button. The selected text will remain highlighted. The computer is now ready to work with this selected text.

Highlighting Your Text: Step by Step Instructions

1. **Position the mouse at the end of the desired text.**
2. **Click and hold down the left mouse button.**
3. **Move the mouse to the beginning of the desired text.**
4. **Release the mouse button.**

Highlighting Your Text: Visual Guide

The Web Wise Seniors' About WWS Page.

Scroll down to locate the end of the second paragraph.

Step 1: Position the mouse at the end of the desired text.

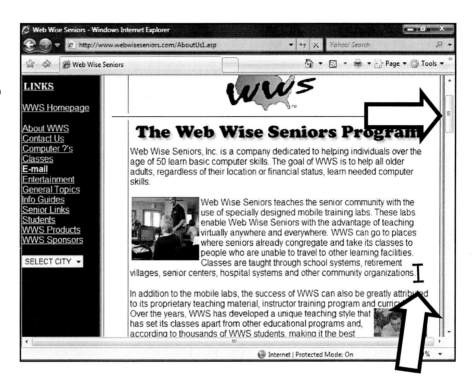

Step 2: Click and hold down the left mouse button.

Step 3:
Move the mouse
to the beginning
of the desired
text.

Step 3: (cont.)
Move the mouse
to the beginning
of the desired
text.

Step 4:
Release the
mouse button.

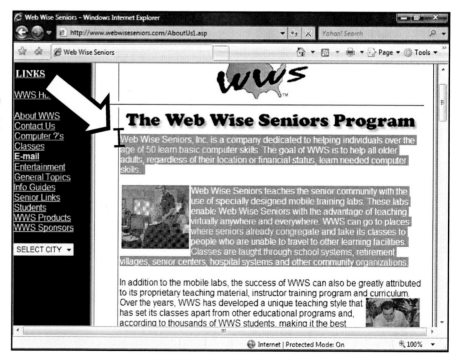

After the text is highlighted, you will be able to copy the text into the computer's temporary memory and then paste it into a new area. This is called copying and pasting.

Chapter 13: Saving from the Internet!

Copying and Pasting

During the copying and pasting process, the computer places a copy of the highlighted text into a temporary holding area called the Clipboard. Once you have opened the word processor, you can insert the text into the new document.

After the paragraphs have been highlighted, click on the PAGE button located on the command bar. Find and click on COPY. The menu will close. It will seem like nothing happened, but the computer has placed a copy of the highlighted text into its temporary memory. Next, open the word processing program and select the PASTE option, which is located under the EDIT menu if you are using Office 97 – 2003 or on the left side of the HOME ribbon if you are using Office 2007.

Copying and Pasting: Step by Step Instructions

1. Highlight the text you want to copy.
2. Click on the PAGE button.
3. Click the COPY option.
4. Open the word processing program and place your blinking cursor where you want the copied text to be located.
   a. Open the START menu.
   b. Click the ALL PROGRAMS option.
   c. Highlight the MICROSOFT OFFICE option.
   d. Click the MICROSOFT OFFICE WORD 2007 option. A blank piece of paper will open on your computer screen.
5. Click on the PASTE option located on the main ribbon.

Copying and Pasting: Visual Guide

Step 1:
Highlight the text you want to copy.

Step 2:
Click on the PAGE button.

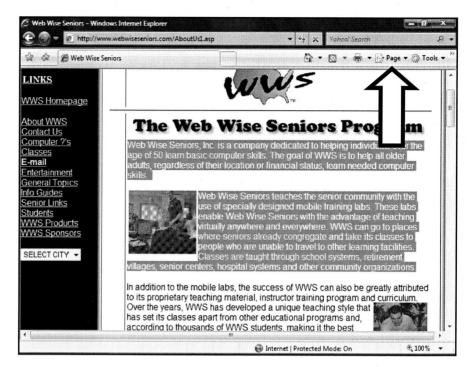

Step 3:
Click the COPY option.

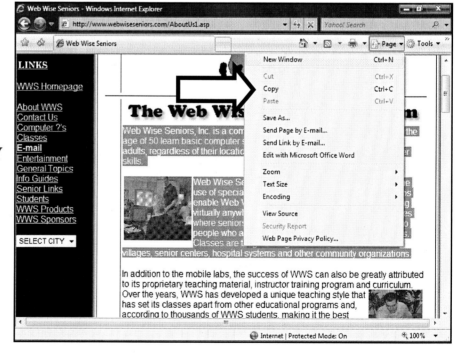

The text has been successfully copied to the computer clipboard.

Step 4: Open the Word Processing program and paste the highlighted selection into the Word document.

Step 4a: Open the START Menu.

Step 4b: Click the ALL PROGRAMS option.

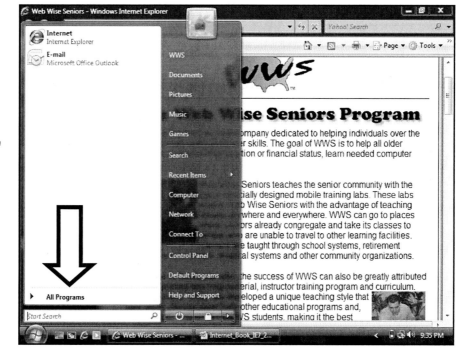

**Step 4c:
Click the
MICROSOFT
OFFICE
option.**

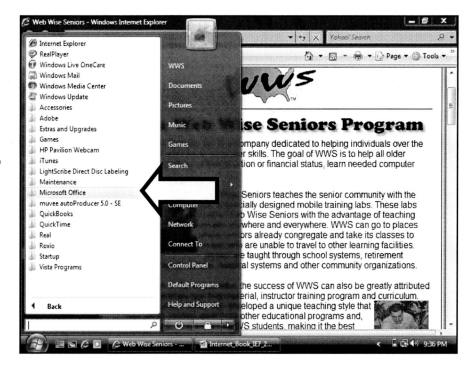

**Step 4d:
Click the
MICROSOFT
OFFICE
WORD 2007
option.**

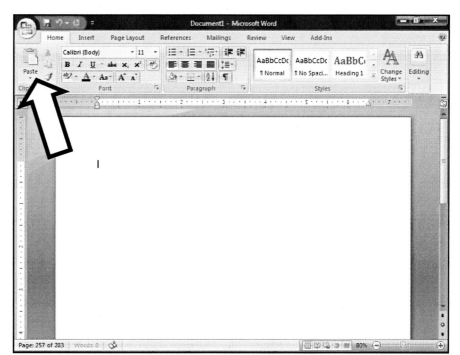

**Step 5:
Click on the
PASTE button.**

**The text has
been pasted in
to the new,
blank Word
document.**

Chapter 13: Saving from the Internet!

Saving the Document

Once you have pasted the new text into the Word Document, you will need to save the document. Position the mouse arrow on the OFFICE button located at the top of the word processing window. Click the left mouse button once to open the menu. Move the mouse arrow down to the "SAVE AS" option and click the left mouse button. This will close the file menu and open the save screen. There are three additional steps to complete the save process. First, you must choose where to save the file. Second, you have to give the file a name. Third, you must click the SAVE button.

Saving Your Work: Step by Step Instructions

1. **Click the OFFICE button.**
2. **Click the option SAVE AS.**
3. **Locate the SAVE IN box and make sure "Documents" is displayed.**
4. **Locate the FILE NAME box and type the name of your document.**
5. **Click the SAVE button.**

Saving Your Work: Visual Guide

Step 1: Click the OFFICE button.

Step 2:
Click the option
SAVE AS.

Step 3:
Locate the
SAVE IN box.
Make sure the
folder
"Documents" is
displayed in the
box.

Step 4:
Locate the
FILE NAME
box and type
the name of
your document.

File Name:
Text Example

Step 5:
Click the SAVE
button.

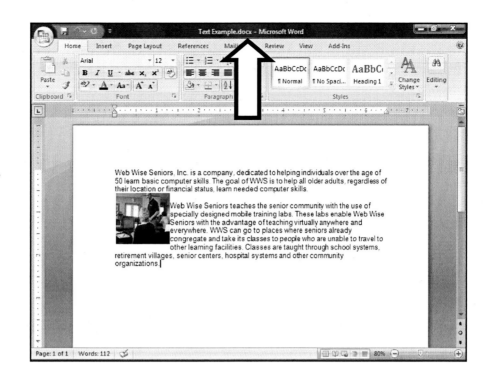

Successfully saved document.

QUESTION: How do you know the file was saved successfully?

ANSWER: Look in the title bar of the program window (your document.) You will see the name of the document displayed in the title bar. This tells you the letter was saved correctly. In this example, the name in the title bar will have changed from "Document4" to "Text Example."

Chapter 13: Saving from the Internet!

Chapter 14

Privacy on the Internet!

What You Will Learn in this Chapter
- ✓ Privacy on the Internet
- ✓ The Safety of Purchasing Items on the Internet

Section 33: Internet Privacy

Take a moment and think of your computer as a car. When you want to drive on the road, you have to go to the license bureau and get a license plate. Once your car has plates, you can drive freely on the road. The public does not know who you are, but can see the license plate. If a person wanted to attempt find out information about you, they would have to write down your license plate number and contact the license bureau. The license bureau will not disclose your personal information unless the person requesting the information is a member of law enforcement. So, to most people, you are just another car on the road represented by a license plate number.

The Internet is set up in a similar fashion. When you connect to the Internet, your ISP gives your computer a unique number called an IP address. This number distinguishes your computer from all of the others on the Internet. Your ISP is the only one who knows the number representing your computer. As an added bonus, every time you get connected, the ISP gives you a new number, making it even more difficult for others to track your Internet travels.

So, how does a hacker (information thief) get your information? The answer to this question relates to the information you have previously entered into your computer. When you first set up your computer, you were asked to type in your name. After the initial setup, other programs might have required additional information. For instance, a financial program might have requested the name of the bank you use and your account information. This information is stored in the computer's memory allowing the program to access it as needed. If the computer did not store the information, you would have to type the information in every time you used the financial program.

It is also common for websites to ask you to supply information about yourself. This enables the website to customize itself to better serve you. The website stores all this information on your computer in something called a cookie. The next time you go to the website, the website will look for this specific cookie as it loads the page. If the website finds its cookie, it will customize the page for you. Since all of this information is stored on your computer, if someone gets access to your computer, they can attempt to obtain your personal information. That is pretty scary.

So should we be worried? The answer is NOT REALLY. Even if a hacker intends to steal a person's information, the hacker does not know which computer is yours on the Internet. This means the hacker has to find you among the millions of people using the Internet at any one moment. In addition, your information is usually not worth the hassle. Most individuals do not have enough money, information, or power, to warrant the time it takes to steal your information and risk getting caught. Hackers usually target companies.

Why are companies the hackers prime targets? First and foremost, they usually have a lot to lose. Also, many companies have websites which are available to the public. Each website is given a static (non-changing) IP address. A static address is necessary to allow the public access to the information stored on a company's website. Finally, most companies keep their computers connected to the Internet 24/7 (24 hours a day, 7 days a week) giving the hacker more time to try to break into the computer. Overall, hackers are looking for the big fish in the sea, not us minnows.

Buying Products and Services Online

Buying and selling products over the Internet is called e-commerce. Billions of dollars worth of transactions take place via the Internet every year. The U.S. Department of Commerce estimated U.S. retail e-commerce sales for the fourth quarter of 2006 was $33.9 billion, an increase of 25 % from one year before.

Should we be worried when we purchase a product or service online? No, if you are careful to select reputable companies, identity theft should be of little concern. Websites conducting e-commerce use multiple layers of security, the most important of which is called data encryption. Most reputable merchants require a 128-bit Secure Socket Layer connection between the store and your computer browser. Basically this means that every piece of your information is encrypted using a 128-bit key before it is transmitted. It would take a hacker many years to try every possible combination to decipher the data. Most thieves do not want to waste their time getting one number; they want a large volume. Using your credit card online is no riskier than using it over a phone.

How can you be sure you are sending the information over a secure connection? The web browser has many ways of telling you an Internet connection is secure. The first signs of safety can be found in a browser's address bar. The address bar should display "https://" before the website address instead of just http://. You can also look at the bottom of your browser screen. A "padlock" is displayed in the browser status bar (lower right corner of the screen) when a secure connection is made. Finally, the browser will display a warning before you begin an information transfer which may not be secure. If you make sure to notice these signs, you can be relatively certain your information is safe.

Chapter 15

E-mail!

What You Will Learn in this Chapter
- ✓ E-mail
- ✓ Selecting an E-mail Provider
- ✓ E-mail Addresses
- ✓ Reading E-mail
- ✓ Writing E-mail

Section 34: E-mail

E-mail has changed and continues to change the world in which we live. Electronic mail, also known as e-mail, enables people to communicate with others around the world instantly and at absolutely no charge. Whether you need to send a short note or a ten page letter, e-mail is your answer. With just a few quick steps, a message can be sent from your computer to anyone in the world.

E-mail's uses are nearly limitless. In the business world, e-mail is used to communicate with employees, advertise products, provide customer service, and more. On the social side, e-mail is used by relatives and friends, whether separated by only a few houses down the street or thousands of miles around the world, to keep in touch. As you can easily imagine, with such widespread use, e-mail has become the most popular aspect of the Internet. An estimated 80% of computer owners use e-mail to communicate.

Another great aspect of e-mail is that the system is not limited to text messages. E-mail enables users to send everything, from full-color photographs to important tax documents, just as quickly. With a couple clicks of the mouse, birthday pictures, tax returns, receipts, and even tickets purchased for concerts and sporting events can be sent and received within seconds.

The most amazing part of this is that you do not even need to own a computer to use e-mail. Many beginning computer users use their library's computers to access their e-mail. Other people use computers at schools, the homes of family and friends, businesses, or even local senior centers to access their e-mail accounts. As long as you can find a computer connected to the Internet, you can use e-mail.

Selecting an E-mail Provider

Once you are connected to the Internet, you need to decide what e-mail service provider you want to use. You have two basic options available. First, your Internet Service Provider will supply you with an e-mail account.

Chapter 15: E-mail!

If you do not want to use your ISP's e-mail or if you just want a second e-mail address/account, there are many websites on the Internet which offer free e-mail service. Therefore, you can either use the e-mail account supplied by your ISP or sign-up for one of the many free e-mail services available on the Internet.

E-mail Addresses

Just as the United Postal Service requires everyone to have a unique mailing address to deliver mail, e-mail services require everyone to have a unique e-mail address. E-mail addresses, instead of being made up of street names, zip codes, and cities, are made up of sign-in names, @ symbols (pronounced AT), e-mail provider names, and Internet extensions such as .org, .com, and .net. A typical e-mail address will look like Johndoe25@Hotmail.com. If you read the preceding e-mail address out loud, it would sound like "John Doe 25 at Hotmail dot com."

If you use your Internet Service Provider for e-mail, the username you selected during setup will be the first part of the e-mail address. After the username is the @ (at) symbol followed by the ISP's name and extension.

Reading an E-mail Message

When you open your e-mail mailbox, called the inbox, the computer will provide a list of any received messages. The list will include who sent the message, the subject, date, and size of the message. From the list of messages, you can use the mouse to open a specific message.

E-mail Inbox.

Once you have opened a message, it will appear in the read screen. Located at the top of the message is the "Message Header." The message header provides you with information about the message. The header includes who the message is FROM, the DATE the message was originally received, who the message was sent TO, and the SUBJECT of the message.

Below the header is the main message. The message can be a few words or a few pages in length depending on how much the sender wrote. After reading the message, you have the option to move to the next message in the mailbox, delete the current message, reply to the sender, or forward the message to someone else.

- **Reply** -- Send a message back to the person who sent the message you are currently reading.

- **Reply All** – Send a message to everyone that received the message you are currently reading.

- **Forward** – Send the exact same message you are currently reading to another person.

Chapter 15: E-mail!

**E-mail
Read Screen.**

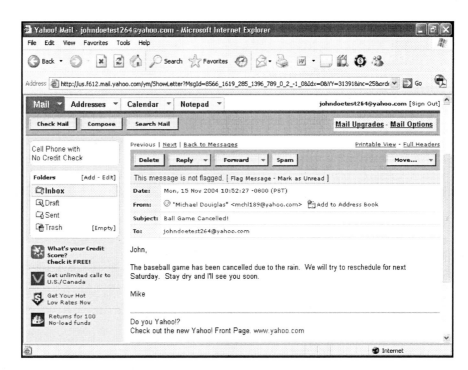

Writing an E-mail Message

If you want to compose and send an e-mail message, you can do that as well. Once you have told the computer you want to write a message, a screen will open, commonly called a compose screen, which will provide input boxes for each part of the new message. The compose screen has four main components including the TO: line, SUBJECT line, message box, and the SEND button.

The TO: line tells your e-mail service where to send your message. It works just like the delivery address on an "old fashioned" letter. Without the postal address, the post office cannot send your letter. Without an address in the TO: line, your e-mail system cannot send the e-mail message. You need to make sure you put in a person's entire e-mail address. This address goes in the TO: line, for example, JohnDoe25@Hotmail.com. Messages sent with partial or incorrect e-mail addresses will be returned.

CAUTION: If an e-mail is returned to you and the e-mail address looks correct, check your "dots." It is very easy to accidentally insert a comma instead of a period, and it is very difficult to tell the difference. JohnDoe25@Hotmail,com looks very similar to JohnDoe25@Hotmail.com. Accidentally using a comma instead of a period is a very common mistake.

After inserting the e-mail address, click in the "SUBJECT" line to activate the blinking cursor and type in the subject of your message. The "SUBJECT" line is important because it provides the person receiving the message with an idea of what the message is about. For example, if you are sending a friend a message about your trip to Europe, a good subject would be "European Vacation."

The subject line of each message will be displayed in the receiver's inbox. A good, descriptive subject line will be appreciated by the receiver of the message. It helps to identify the contents of messages without forcing the reader to look at the entire message. Messages sent without subjects will automatically have "N/A" inserted in the subject line.

After filling in the To: line and the SUBJECT line, the next step is to write your text message. Every "New Message" screen will have a large white box near the middle or bottom of the screen. Click anywhere within this large white box to activate the blinking cursor. Type as much as you like. The message box will expand to fit long messages. A scroll bar will appear to help you move up and down your message.

When you are finished typing the message, click the SEND button to distribute the message to the recipients.

We've given you the e-mail basics above. There is so much additional information relating to e-mail that we've published a book specifically to address e-mail.

Chapter 15: E-mail!

E-mail Compose Screen.

Chapter 15: E-mail!

Chapter 16

Internet Yellow Pages!

What You Will Learn in this Chapter
✓ A list of popular websites
(Note: Website addresses are subject to change without notice.)

Section 35:   Internet Yellow Pages

- **Anti–Virus**
  - o MacAfee - www.mcafee.com
  - o Norton - www.symantec.com

- **Auctions**
  - o Amazon - auctions.amazon.com
  - o Ebay - www.ebay.com
  - o Yahoo - auctions.yahoo.com

- **Books**
  - o Amazon - www.amazon.com
  - o Barnes & Noble - www.barnesandnoble.com
  - o Borders - www.borders.com

- **Computers**
  - o Apple - www.apple.com
  - o Dell - www.dell.com
  - o Gateway - www.gateway.com
  - o Sony - www.sony.com
  - o Hewlett Packard - www.hp.com

- **Computer Training**
  - o Web Wise Seniors - www.webwiseseniors.com

- **Electronics**
  - o Best Buy - www.bestbuy.com
  - o Circuit City - www.circuitcity.com

- **Employment**
  - o Career Board - www.careerboard.com
  - o Monster - www.monster.com

Chapter 16: Internet Yellow Pages!

- **Financial**
    - Cbs.marketwatch - www.Cbs.marketwatch.com
    - American Stock Exchange (AMEX) - www.amex.com
    - Morningstar - www.Morningstar.com
    - Nasdaq Stock Market - www.nasdaq.com
    - New York Stock Exchange (NYSE) - www.nyse.com

- **Games**
    - Games - www.games.com
    - MSN Game Zone - zone.msn.com
    - Pogo - www.pogo.com
    - PopCap Games - www.popcap.com
    - Shockwave - www.shockwave.com
    - Yahoo! Games - games.yahoo.com

- **Greeting Cards**
    - 123greetings - www.123greetings.com
    - American Greetings - www.americangreetings.com
    - Blue Mountain - www.bluemountain.com
    - Hallmark - www.hallmark.com
    - Regards - www.regards.com

- **Home Improvement**
    - Home Depot - www.homedepot.com
    - Lowes - www.lowes.com

- **Instant Messenger Programs**
    - AOL - www.aol.com
    - MSN - www.msn.com
    - Yahoo - www.yahoo.com

- **Maps and Directions**
    - Expedia - www.expedia.com
    - Mapquest - www.mapquest.com
    - Yahoo Maps - maps.yahoo.com

- **Medical**
  - o Eli Lilly - www.lilly.com
  - o GlaxoSmithKline - us.gsk.com
  - o Johnson & Johnson - www.jnj.com
  - o Merck & Co. - www.merck.com
  - o Pfizer - www.pfizer.com
  - o WebMd - www.webmd.com

- **Movies**
  - o Blockbuster - www.blockbuster.com
  - o Hollywood Video - www.hollywoodvideo.com
  - o Moviefone - www.moviefone.com
  - o Movies.com - www.movies.com

- **Music**
  - o Billboard - www.billboard.com
  - o iTunes.com - www.itunes.com
  - o MTV - www.mtv.com
  - o VH1 - www.vh1.com

- **Newspapers**
  - o Cleveland Plain Dealer -www.cleveland.com
  - o Los Angeles Times - www.latimes.com
  - o New York Times - www.nytimes.com
  - o USA Today - www.usatoday.com
  - o Washington Post - www.washingtonpost.com
  - o Wall Street Journal - www.wsj.com

- **Search Engines**
  - o AltaVista - www.altavista.com
  - o Excite - www.excite.com
  - o Google - www.google.com
  - o Lycos - www.lycos.com
  - o Yahoo – www.yahoo.com

- **Shopping**
  - Home Shopping Network - www.hsn.com
  - QVC - www.qvc.com
  - REI - ww.REI.com
  - Walmart - www.walmart.com

- **Software**
  - Adobe - www.adobe.com
  - QuickBooks/Quicken - www.intuit.com
  - Microsoft - www.microsoft.com
  - WinZip - www.winzip.com

- **Sports**
  - ESPN - espn.go.com
  - FOX Sports - www.foxsports.com
  - Sporting News.com - www.sportingnews.com
  - Yahoo! Sports - sports.yahoo.com

- **Travel**
  - CheapTickets - www.CheapTickets.com
  - Expedia - www.Expedia.com
  - Hotels - www.hotels.com
  - ORBITZ - www.ORBITZ.com
  - Priceline - www.priceline.com
  - Travelocity - www.travelocity.com

- **Toys**
  - KB Toys - www.kbtoys.com
  - Fisher-Price - www.fisherprice.com
  - Toys "R" Us - www.toysrus.com

- **Weather**
  - National Weather Service - www.nws.noaa.gov
  - Weather Channel - www.weather.com

- **White/Yellow Pages**
  - Verizon Super Pages - www.bigyellow.com
  - Yellow.com - www.yellow.com

Index!

Index!

Appendix!

Thank you for using the Web Wise Seniors' Internet for Beginners book. We hope you enjoyed learning with it. Please let us know what you think of the book. If you found it easy to use and enjoyed the learning experience, please tell your family and friends.

Feel free to send your comments and feedback
to us at the following address:

Web Wise Seniors, Inc.
305 Woodstock Rd.
Eastlake, Ohio 44095

Or E-mail us at
WWS@WebWiseSeniors.com

Thank You!

Appendix!

Web Wise Seniors is Proud to Present...
The "for Beginners" Series

	Title	Subtitle	ISBN #
Book	Basic Computers for Beginners	Windows XP	1-933404-45-0
Book	Basic Computers for Beginners	Windows Vista	1-933404-46-9
Book	Basic Internet for Beginners	Internet Explorer 7	1-933404-47-7
Book	Basic Email for Beginners		1-933404-48-5
Book	Microsoft Word 2007 for Beginners	Microsoft Word 2007	1-933404-49-3
Book	Microsoft Excel 2007 for Beginners	Microsoft Excel 2007	1-933404-50-7
Book	Microsoft Word for Beginners	Microsoft Word 2003	1-933404-51-5
Book	Microsoft Excel for Beginners	Microsoft Word 2003	1-933404-52-3
	Large Print Books are $34.95 each.		
	To Order Call Toll Free: 1-866-232-7032		

	Title	Subtitle	ISBN #
Windows Vista Series			
DVD	Basic Computers Part 1 VISTA	Introduction for Beginners	1-933404-54-X
DVD	Basic Computers Part 2 VISTA	Essentials of the Keyboard	1-933404-55-8
DVD	Basic Computers Part 3 VISTA	Filing Fundamentals	1-933404-56-6
DVD	Basic Computers Part 4 VISTA	Customizing Your Computer	1-933404-57-4
DVD	The Internet Part 1 IE7	Searching the Internet	1-933404-58-2
DVD	The Internet Part 2 IE7	Better Searching Techniques	1-933404-59-0
DVD	E-mail Part 1 Windows Mail	The Basics	1-933404-60-4
DVD	E-mail Part 1 Windows Mail	Advanced Techniques	1-933404-61-2
Windows XP Series			
DVD	Basic Computers Part 1 XP	Introduction for Beginners	1-933404-74-4
DVD	Basic Computers Part 2 XP	Essentials of the Keyboard	1-933404-75-2
DVD	Basic Computers Part 3 XP	Filing Fundamentals	1-933404-76-0
DVD	Basic Computers Part 4 XP	Customizing Your Computer	1-933404-77-9
DVD	The Internet Part 1 IE6	Searching the Internet	1-933404-78-7
DVD	The Internet Part 2 IE6	Better Searching Techniques	1-933404-79-5
DVD	E-mail Part 1 Outlook Express	The Basics	1-933404-80-9
DVD	E-mail Part 2 Outlook Express	Advanced Techniques	1-933404-81-7

<u>Additional Titles on the Next Page</u>

Appendix!

Web Wise Seniors is Proud to Present...
The "for Beginners" Series

	Title	Subtitle	ISBN #
Microsoft Office 2007 Series			
DVD	Word 2007 Part 1	An Introduction to Word Processing	1-933404-62-0
DVD	Word 2007 Part 2	Essential Word Tools	1-933404-63-9
DVD	Excel 2007 Part 1	An Introduction to Spreadsheets	1-933404-64-7
DVD	Excel 2007 Part 2	Essential Tools	1-933404-65-5
Microsoft Office 2003 Series			
DVD	Word Part 1	An Introduction to Word Processing	1-933404-82-5
DVD	Word Part 2	Essential Word Tools	1-933404-83-3
DVD	Word Part 3	Bullets and Numbers	1-933404-84-1
DVD	Word Part 4	Mail Merge and More	1-933404-85-X
DVD	Excel Part 1	An Introduction to Spreadsheets	1-933404-86-8
DVD	Excel Part 2	Essential Tools	1-933404-87-6
DVD	PowerPoint Part 1	Creating a Presentation	1-933404-88-4
DVD	PowerPoint Part 2	Transitions and More	1-933404-89-2
DVD	Publisher Part 1	An Introduction to Publisher	1-933404-90-6
DVD	Publisher Part 2	Utilize the Power of Publisher	1-933404-91-4
DVD	Outlook Part 1	An Introduction to Outlook	1-933404-92-2
DVD	Outlook Part 2	The Tools of Outlook	1-933404-93-0
Spanish DVD Series			
DVD	Basic Computers XP Part 1	Introduction for Beginners	1-933404-67-1
DVD	Basic Computers Vista Part 1	Introduction for Beginners	1-933404-66-3
DVD	Basic Computers Vista Part 2	Essentials of the Keyboard	1-933404-70-1
DVD	Basic Computers Vista Part 3	Filing Fundamentals	1-933404-71-X
DVD	The Internet IE7 Part 1	Searching the Internet	1-933404-68-X
DVD	E-mail Windows Mail Part 1	The Basics	1-933404-69-8
DVD	Word 2007 Part 1	An Introduction to Word Processing	1-933404-72-8
DVD	Excel 2007 Part 1	An Introduction to Spreadsheets	1-933404-73-6
DVDs are $19.95 each.			
To Order Call Toll Free: 1-866-232-7032			

Appendix!

<u>Notes:</u>

Appendix!

<u>Notes:</u>